Listening to Our Grandmothers' Stories

WINNER OF THE 1998

NORTH AMERICAN INDIAN PROSE AWARD

Award Committee

Gerald Vizenor, Chairman

University of California at Berkeley

Diane Glancy

Macalester College

A. LaVonne Brown Ruoff

University of Illinois at Chicago

Listening to Our Grandmothers' Stories

THE BLOOMFIELD ACADEMY FOR

CHICKASAW FEMALES,

1852–1949

❀

Amanda J. Cobb

❀

University of Nebraska Press

Lincoln and London

❀

⊗

Library of Congress Cataloging-in-Publication Data
Cobb, Amanda J., 1970–
Listening to our grandmother's stories:
the Bloomfield Academy for Chickasaw
Females, 1852–1949 / Amanda J. Cobb.
p. cm.
Includes bibliographical references and index.
ISBN 0-8032-1509-6 (cloth: alk. paper)
1. Bloomfield Academy for Chickasaw Females—History.
2. Chickasaw girls—Education.   3. Chickasaw girls—Social conditions.
4. Chickasaw girls—History—Sources.   5. Off-reservation
boarding schools—Oklahoma—History.   I. Title.
E97.6.B55 C63 2000
976.6004'973—dc21   00-036501

FOR ALL OF THOSE WOMEN

WHO ATTENDED BLOOMFIELD ACADEMY

OR CARTER SEMINARY, 1852–1949

Contents

Illustrations

Acknowledgments

This book is the result of several years of thought and study and work—work not done alone, but with and through the help of others. At this time, I offer my appreciation and thanks to those who made the completion of this project possible.

First, I would like to thank the University of Nebraska Press, my doctoral committee at the University of Oklahoma—in particular, my director, Catherine Hobbs—and my colleagues at New Mexico State University for their direction, insight, and support.

I extend my gratitude and love always to the people of the Chickasaw Nation of Oklahoma. I must thank all of the members of Americans for Indian Opportunity, who are both friends and family—participating has been such a gift. I especially need to thank the AIO Ambassador Class of 1998 and the AIO staff and directors, including Dave Beck, Rosalyn LaPier, Laura Harris, and, finally, LaDonna Harris, whose grace and graciousness reaches us all.

I would like to thank the following Oklahoma libraries, museums, and archives and the people who work there for their willingness to help in my search for difficult-to-find documents and materials about Bloomfield: the Ardmore Public Library, Ardmore; Carter Seminary, Ardmore: the Chickasaw Council House Museum, Tishomingo; the Chickasaw Cultural Center Museum Library Archives, Ada; the Chickasaw Historical Society, Ada; the Chickasaw Library, Ardmore; the Chickasaw Library, Davis; the Chickasaw Library, Healdton; the Chickasaw Library, Johnston County, Tishomingo; the Chickasaw Library, Love County, Marietta; the Chickasaw Library, Wilson; the City of Madill Library, Madill; the Edmon Low Library, Oklahoma State University, Stillwater; the Five Civilized Tribes Agency, Muskogee; the Greater Southwest Historical Museum, Ardmore; the Henry G. Bennett Memorial Library, Southeastern Oklahoma State University, Durant; the Love County Historical Society, Marietta; the Oklahoma Historical Society, Oklahoma City; the Robert L. Williams Public Library, Durant; the State Department of Education, Oklahoma City; and the Western History Collection, University of Oklahoma, Norman. In addition, I am grateful to staff at the Denison Public Library, Denison, Texas, and the Federal Records Center, Fort Worth, Texas, for their assistance.

I especially want to thank my aunt, Murielene Cobb Potts, for providing me with the school memorabilia of my grandma, Ida Mae Pratt Cobb, items that, for me, mark the beginning of the story. I also thank Pauline Williford Adkins, Fanny Hughes Bass, Jeanne Liddell Cochran, Clara Pittman Gatlin, Dorothy Wall Holt, Leona Williford Isaac, Betty Ruth Kemp, Claudine Williford King, Hettie McCauley King, Ida Bell Hughes Martin, Mary Pittman Parris, Frances Griffin Robinson, Fannye Williford Skaggs, Juanita Keel Tate, Ula Mae Pittman Welch, and Ora Lee Chuculate Woods for sharing their stories with me.

I want to thank my grandparents, Ida Mae Pratt Cobb, Trueman C. Cobb, Clara Holt Byrd, and E. Wayne Byrd, who are not with me now and can never read this, but who are part of me still and part of this book.

Finally, I would like to say thank you to my mother, Patricia Cobb, not only for her patience, her interest and assistance, and her tireless work researching and reading, but for creating a home where I was able to find "excellent things in women."

To my family, whose understanding and love sustain me: my sister, Elizabeth Cobb McCraw; my brother-in-law, Shannon McCraw; my daddy, John G. Cobb; my mother, Patricia J. Cobb—*How can I thank you enough?*

Note to Readers

I would like to explain my use of certain terms that
appear throughout this book. I have used specific tribal
names whenever possible, for example, Chickasaw,
Choctaw, and so on. When referring to American
Indian tribes and people more generally, I have used the
terms *American Indian, Native American, Native,* and *Indian*
interchangeably, although I tend to prefer the terms
American Indian and *Indian.* I sometimes use the term
tribal nations to highlight the sovereignty of individual
American Indian tribes.

I use the term *mixed-blood* to refer to people of mixed
Indian and white heritage. The term *full-blood* refers to
people having Indian ancestry only. I do not use either
term to make value judgments about "how Indian"
individuals are, a question that is always inappropriate,
or how "traditional" or "progressive" individuals are,
which is not necessarily a question of blood.

Introduction
Iposi immih (For Grandma)

✱

Well, you missed a lot because she was a fine person.
And a lot of fun. — HETTIE MCCAULEY KING *on Ida Mae Pratt Cobb (Dinah)*

As I look back over the past few years, I see books, thoughts, even lines of poetry that intrigued me to such an extent that they became part of my consciousness. And though the ideas did not seem particularly connected at the time, they eventually gave rise to this project and have shaped it and given it meaning. If I had to discuss the ideas and name them, I would call them *continuance*—the remembrance of times, places, and people; the knowing of those times, places, and people through imaginative acts; and finally, the going on, the telling of the stories.

This book has personal significance. It is not unusual for Native authors to write about personal subjects; many have done so. This is an act of continuance. Of special note is Simon Ortiz (Acoma), who, in his beautifully crafted introduction to *Woven Stone*, writes, "[The Acoma stories] tied me into the communal body of my people and heritage . . . when I learned to read and write, I believe I felt those stories continued somehow in the new language, and use of the new language and they would never be lost, forgotten, and finally gone. They would always continue."[1]

I agree with Ortiz, who states, "Continuance . . . is life itself."[2] Two other authors, in particular, stand out in my mind: Maurice Kenny (Mohawk) and N. Scott Momaday (Kiowa). I feel I must mention them here because their work has influenced the writing of this book in important ways.

In *Tekonwatonti/Molly Brant*, Maurice Kenny gives life to Mohawk leader Molly Brant (1735–95) by telling her story in a series of personae poems. He writes in his introduction that American Indian women have too often been left out of history books, that his purpose is to write a revisionary history of sorts; his poetry, however, does so much more than that. Part of one poem in particular always strikes me:

> I've never given them much thought.
> They've entered and left
> playing such a small role
> in my imaginings,
> but they are my history,
> veins and tongue,
> are cousins, grandparents.
>
> *I believe in dreams.*
>
> . . .
>
> I am not frightened,
> but pleased they have entered my shadow.
> I will knock on doors and windowpanes.
> I will sleep them into my embrace.
> I will open my veins for their blood.[3]

In the epilogue, Kenny writes, "There is a need to touch."[4] Although this phrase is brief, it says a great deal. *Molly Brant* is Kenny's attempt to touch, to reach through time and touch the past and know Molly personally.

Other lines I cannot forget come from Scott Momaday's autobiographical narrative, *The Names*. Momaday, like Kenny, uses an imaginative process to develop personal relationships. Of his mother, he writes, "Some of my mother's memories have become my own. This is the real burden of blood; this is immortality."[5] He uses an imaginative process again when he describes his relationship with his grandfather in the following lines: "Mammedaty was my grandfather, whom I never knew. Yet he came to be imagined posthumously in the going on of the blood. . . . He enters into my dreams; he persists in his name."[6]

As I mentioned, this book has personal significance for me; it is about the Bloomfield Academy for Chickasaw Females (1852–1949), a boarding school that my grandmother, Ida Mae Pratt Cobb (Dinah) attended in 1924–26. The research began when my Aunt Murielene gave me Grandma's report cards, scrapbook, and pictures from her time at Bloomfield. Specifically, this project is a memorial to her. She was born in 1907, the year of Oklahoma statehood, and died in 1978, when I was seven years old. Although I knew her briefly as a grandmother, I never really had the chance to know her as a person. Many details of her life I have gleaned through stories told by my father, my aunt, my grandpa, and others, friends and relatives in her community who knew her. By all accounts, she was "a great favorite." She was certainly a favorite of mine when I was seven. She died suddenly on Monday, May 22, 1978. Just two days before her death, she attended the annual Bloomfield reunion for the first time. In May of 1996, I had the privilege of attending the Bloomfield reunion, where I spoke to the women about the plans for my research. I was sitting in the middle of the back row, next to the center aisle. Juanita Tate, a family friend, distant relative, and fellow historian, was sitting on my right. As I addressed the women, Juanita, known for her quiet, soft-spoken manner and reserve, stood up and told me that she had just remembered something. On May 20, 1978, she had been sitting on the right side of my grandma, who was sitting in the middle of the back row, next to the center aisle. I thanked her for sharing that with me, and I thank her again.

This book is not a collection of poetry like Maurice Kenny's or an autobiographical narrative like Scott Momaday's. It is a scholarly, historical narrative. Nonetheless, there is a need to touch, and this book is an attempt to know my grandma better, to reach through time, to listen to and touch the past. In my search through archives for documents, data, pictures, and memorabilia, I search for Grandma. When I listen to relatives and other women who attended the academy, I am, in a sense, listening to her. This book is *iposi immih*—for Grandma. It is also for all of the women who attended Bloomfield, whose accounts made this book possible. I cannot begin without thanking them for their time, energy, and kindnesses. I am lucky to have known them, and I hope that this work is something that they will be proud to have been a part of. Many of them are someone's grandma.

I

Nananumpolit aiya (To Start to Tell a Story)
Literacy and Schooling

✳

Thus, the one room schoolhouse, with the proverbial schoolmarm standing in the doorway as a symbol of literacy and civilization, was one of the first landmarks of a western community. — DAVID WALLACE ADAMS, *Education for Extinction*

Beginnings

Indian Territory, circa 1850. The story goes that Reverend John Harpole Carr of the Methodist Episcopal Church pitched a tent in a field of flowers. He was full of missionary zeal and missionary love, and he had a vision — a vision of a schoolhouse rising there out of the wildflowers. It was to be a schoolhouse for Chickasaw girls, a boarding school. He would build it and maintain it and grow orchards and raise animals to sustain it. He would superintend, and his wife, Angelina, would teach. He could not know that the terrible war soon to come would halt the progress of the school and work of the missionaries. He could not know that in time the school would become the cultural seat of Indian Territory, the pride of the Chickasaw Nation. He could not know of the fires that would destroy it again and again, and he could not know of the great desire of the Chickasaw people to rebuild and begin again and again. Did he imagine, there in the field of flowers, the struggles for control that would ensue, or what would be at stake in those struggles? Or did his hopes for the school outweigh all other thoughts — hopes firmly rooted in the ideology of literacy and all it would bring: salvation, civilization, nationalism, individualism, prosperity. . . . Imagine, John and Angelina making plans into the night, talking, eating, telling stories, and laughing with the Chickasaw families so anxious to see the school built. Imagine the little girls wondering what it would be like to go to the school, excited perhaps, perhaps homesick already. Imagine the Carrs, the Chickasaw families, and the daughters, all looking at the field of flowers, watching a schoolhouse rise up out of the field, each with a particular vision of what it would become. It was to that field that former Chickasaw chief Jackson Kemp mailed a letter to his friend John Carr, who was camping there. He did not know how to address the letter. Remembering the wildflowers covering the prairie, he wrote on the envelope "Bloomfield." So the story goes.

The Bloomfield Academy for Chickasaw Females opened its doors to twenty-five students in the fall of 1852. Originally located near what is now Achille, Oklahoma, approximately fifteen miles south of Durant, Bloomfield suffered several fires and in 1914 was relocated to the site of the Old Hargrove College in Ardmore, Oklahoma. The school was renamed Carter Seminary in 1932 and continued functioning as a boarding school for girls until 1949, at which time boys were admitted. Four years later, the school officially closed its doors as an academy when all of the children were integrated into the Ardmore Public Schools. The children continued to board at Carter, however, and Carter Seminary is still in operation as a boarding facility for American Indian children today.

The story of Bloomfield is remarkable for many reasons, the most significant being its very difference from other boarding schools for Native American children. The school was founded by the Chickasaw Nation in conjunction with missionaries in 1852, a time when many tribes were still the objects of massive military campaigns. Bloomfield reached its zenith as an academy in the last years of the nineteenth century, a time when the federal government was waging a new sort of war against Indians.

Although the Chickasaw people had been forcibly removed from their homeland in Mississippi to Indian Territory and had suffered devastating loss, illness, and deaths as a result, they had not been subjugated to a reservation, a fate met by many tribes. The federal government's decision to force Indian nations on to reservations signified a major change in American Indian policy. The United States had previously dealt with American Indian tribes either by making treaties or waging war, both of which were based on their recognition of each tribe as a sovereign power. The reservation system did not merely represent a change in policy; it represented a fundamental change in the government's perception of Indian peoples. No longer would government officials view Indian tribes as independent nations. Now, policymakers chose to see tribes as wards of the government, colonized peoples, and constructed policy built on that belief, thus leveling a major blow to American Indian people.[1] Once the Civil War ended, the U.S. government and its citizens again turned their full attention to the conquest of the western frontier. No opposing force could halt the steady march of white settlers in their advance or hold back the building of the railroads, "which tied the nation together with ever tightening bands of steel."[2] U.S. citizens, anchored in and acting out of the spirit of American Evangelicalism, believed their conquest of the West, both physical and spiritual, was more than inevitable; it was divine.[3] Truly, America believed, this war was holy.

As a result, legislators began to see the reservation policy as a quick solution for pressing problems. The reservation system, which was less expensive and more humane than military solutions, would cement the conceptualization of Indians as wards of the government yet would be a natural extension of previous, less comprehensive removal policies.[4] On a practical level, forcing Indian peoples onto reservations (1) provided more land for white settlement; (2) segregated Indians and whites, allowing white settlers to move westward and protecting both from the possible violence of the other; and (3) served the "humanitarian" purpose of providing a safe place where Indians could become "civilized" without disruption.[5] Soon, however, as white settlements hemmed in the reservations on every side and white settlers clamored for more land, reservation land, the government realized that the reservation system had only been a temporary solution to the land issue and had actually created a new and very real set of problems.[6] Reservations reinforced the very communal, tribal systems the federal government wanted to smash. In addition, by removing Indian peoples from their homelands and taking away their self-sufficiency, legislators had created a system of dependency and poverty.[7] Finally, white settlers wanted more land, indeed, believed it was their Manifest Destiny to have the land, and neither the United States government nor its citizenry would rest until every single acre of land was open for white settlement. This opinion was shared by Christian reformers. General Clinton B. Fisk, president of the 1885 Lake Mohonk Conference of Friends of the Indian, voiced the principle objective underpinning the conference's reform policy: "We should work especially to throw down every barrier in the country, so as to have no foot of land on which any American may not go."[8] Legislators needed new answers and new policies quickly. They did not have to look far.

American Indian policy was at this time heavily influenced by the efforts of several Indian reform groups who, united in their belief that the U.S. treatment of American Indians constituted a stain on the honor of the new republic, demanded new solutions to the "Indian problem" that had plagued the country since its inception.[9] The "New Christian Reformers" were well-educated, well-established, well-intentioned, evangelical Protestants who had various levels of experience with Indian issues.[10] Unfortunately, they had little to no actual knowledge of Indian people or their values and worldview and no interest in finding out what Indians thought about their own situation.[11] They gathered annually, beginning in 1883, at the Lake Mohonk Conference of Friends of the Indian in order to agree upon a reform platform and to decide how best to influence the legislature and public opinion.[12] The influence they wielded cannot be underestimated. According to historian Francis Paul Prucha, "they represented or reflected a powerful and predominant segment of Protestant church membership, and thereby of late nineteenth-century American society. When they spoke, they spoke for a large majority of the nation. . . . They were the chief channel through which this Americanism came to bear upon the Indians."[13]

The reform groups did not always agree precisely how Indian policies should be reformed; they did, however, agree on the basic answer to the "Indian question." Their answer was "Civilization," thought of as simultaneously a benevolent gift and a new battle to be fought. The breaking up of reservations for the allotment of land in severalty and the extension of the nation's legal system to Indians were both parts of the reformers' plan to civilize American Indians; however, reformers believed that "true civilization" depended on more than land and law. True civilization required real cultural change — changes in government, in family systems, in habitation, in livelihood, in values, in dress. Civilization required Christianity. Civilization required the English language. The reformers believed that only one system could accomplish such complete change. Civilization, the reformers concurred, was a matter of education, of literacy. The American common school that rose to dominance in the United States as the "one best" educational system was considered the glory of the new republic, the panacea for every ill, and reformers had every faith in its civilizing powers.[14] Christian education was a natural outgrowth of the nation's ongoing missionary endeavors out west and, furthermore, was much more economical than either warfare or perpetual dependency.[15] Education was considered a long-term strategy; it was aimed, after all, at children. Providing Indian children with formal education would realize a sweeping progressive victory, and since reformers believed that schooling would speed the slow "cultural evolution" process, perhaps transforming the Indians from their current stage of "barbarism" to the ultimate stage of "civilization" in a single generation, the victory would be won in record time.[16] According to Merrill Gates, the president of the 1891 Lake Mohonk Conference for Indian reform: "That is the army that is going to win the victory. We are going to conquer barbarism; but we are going to do it by getting at the barbarians one by one. We are going to do it by that conquest of the individual man, woman, and child which leads to the truest civilization. We are going to conquer the Indians by a standing army of school-teachers armed with ideas, winning victories by industrial training, and by the gospel of love and the gospel of work." [17] During this time period, children of many tribes were literally ripped away from their families and forced to attend federally run reservation and off-reservation boarding schools, the latter considered the most effective. Unfortunately, stories told by students of these schools are never happy ones. [18]

But Bloomfield was different. The Chickasaws had not been relegated to a reservation and had achieved in the last half of the century in Indian Territory a much higher level of autonomy, self-sufficiency, and independence than most other tribal nations. The Chickasaw Nation founded Bloomfield in 1852, thirty-one years before the Christian reformers first gathered at Lake Mohonk. The Chickasaws founded Bloomfield, not because the federal government demanded it, but because the Chickasaw people knew that literacy training was crucial to their survival as a nation, to their preservation. Bloomfield is also remarkable (1) because the Indian academies were far superior to any schooling provided for whites in Indian Territory at that time; (2) because it existed as an academy long after the corresponding Chickasaw academies shut down, long after the demise of the academy system at the hands of the new, uniquely American common school; and, finally, (3) because it was an academy for females.

We have very little knowledge of the history of women's education. According to Catherine Hobbs in the introduction to *Nineteenth-Century Women Learn to Write*, "histories of nineteenth-century education and writing instruction most often generalize from elite male experience, using records of the century's prestigious all-male institutions. . . . The value of having histories of girls' and women's experiences of literacy need not be argued, yet the work of writing these histories and listening to women's 'voices' from our past has only begun." [19]

Sadly, the voices of women are not the only ones excluded from our histories. Histories of education have rarely included American Indian education, and, unfortunately, histories of American Indian education have rarely discussed the special concerns and perspectives of American Indian women. However, there are some scholars who have given voice to an impressive range of perspectives and contexts and who have made many excellent contributions to the field of American Indian education. These scholars have done much to demonstrate the depth, complexity, and symbolic significance of the boarding school experience, an experience that has shaped our identities, nations, and relationships with each other, like it or not.

Of these scholars, a few have contributed to the field by offering broad, comprehensive histories of American Indian education. Among them is Francis Paul Prucha, who has time and again provided thoughtful and thought-provoking histories of American Indian policy and schooling that form a foundation for all scholars of Indian education. Of special note are *American Indian Policy in Crisis: Christian Reformers and the Indian, 1865–1900* and *The Churches and the Indian Schools, 1888–1912*. Another such scholar, Margaret Szasz, in *Education and the American Indian: The Road to Self-Determination since 1928*, provides broad, historical coverage of the education directed by the Indian Bureau between 1928 and 1973, a crucial period in the history of Indian education, marked by the 1928 Meriam Report and the 1969 Kennedy Report. Furthermore, David Wallace Adams not only discusses policy formation and implementation in *Education for Extinction: American Indians and the Boarding School Experience, 1875–1928* but also provides a superb analysis of students' complicated and ambivalent responses to the schooling system. Significantly, Michael Coleman makes students' autobiographical accounts the focus of *American Indian Children at School, 1850–1930*, and, in doing so, unites the voices of a hundred students from different tribes and schools, emphasizing both their collective experience and individual challenges and adding an essential perspective to our histories.

Other scholars have chosen to highlight specific schools, tribes, or students, which allows them to more closely examine the particular context of a school or the intricate dynamics of cultural interaction and identity formation, issues that are at the heart of this book. Furthermore, focusing on specific schools or students has enabled these scholars to feature the oral histories of former students in their studies; their work with oral histories has helped pave the way for my own.

K. Tsianina Lomawaima, Clyde Ellis, and Sally J. McBeth have all deepened their work by interviewing former students and bringing significant firsthand perspectives to the conversation. In *They Called It Prairie Light: The Story of Chilocco Indian School*, K. Tsianina Lomawaima draws on interviews with more than sixty Chilocco alumnae, demonstrating the richness and diversity of student responses to their experiences and underscoring the fact that Indian students were never passive recipients of a system. This book was of particular interest to me because many Bloomfield students went on to attend Chilocco and often speak of their experiences there. Clyde Ellis, in *To Change Them Forever: Indian Education at the Rainy Mountain Boarding School, 1893–1920*, reminds us that change signifies life and strength. Cultures and cultural identities are constantly changing; for the Kiowa people, boarding schools were the "latest in a long series" of changes.[20] Finally, in her insightful work *Ethnic Identity and the Boarding School Experience of West-Central Oklahoma American Indians*, Sally J. McBeth uses interviews to demonstrate that boarding schools became pan-Indian centers where students integrated and forged a strong, common ethnic identity.

Like other authors I have mentioned, Brenda Child describes the boarding school experience from the perspective of the students; however, in *Boarding School Seasons: American Indian Families, 1900–1940*, Child adds an important and unique perspective by sharing the story through the letters of the students and their family members. Another distinctive story is told by Esther Horne and Sally McBeth in *Essie's Story: The Life and Legacy of a Shoshone Teacher*. Horne and McBeth collaborate to tell Horne's own life story, first as a student in the boarding school system and then as a teacher.

All of these histories have been invaluable sources for my own work and have greatly informed this book. However, the schools established by the so-called Five Civilized Tribes of Oklahoma were shaped by very different historical events. As a matter of fact, the experiences of children at Bloomfield and other academies run by the Five Civilized Tribes were so distinctive that in *Education for Extinction*, Adams writes that they are exempt from his study on the grounds that their stories are "sufficiently unique as to require a separate investigation altogether."[21]

Devon Mihesuah undertakes just this sort of investigation in *Cultivating the Rosebuds: The Education of Women at the Cherokee Female Seminary, 1851–1909*. Mihesuah's site-specific archival research discusses the type of education offered at the Cherokee Female Seminary in Indian Territory, in present-day Tahlequah, Oklahoma. Mihesuah's research is particularly relevant to this project because the Cherokees and Chickasaws both belong to the Five Civilized Tribes, that is, southeastern tribes that were removed to Indian Territory in the 1830s. Not only do the tribes share similar backgrounds, but the education of the Cherokee children in Indian Territory began at the same time as the education of the Chickasaw children, and the type of education offered was also similar.

I hope to contribute to the existing scholarship, not by revising or correcting already written histories of literacy instruction, but instead by telling an untold story — adding a thread to the history of women's literacy education, to the type of literacy instruction American Indian students received, and to the special issues of language and identity they faced, particularly mixed-blood students. The experiences of Indian children at boarding schools across the United States during the period of strict federal assimilation policies are quite different than the experiences of white children. Furthermore, American Indian tribes are not identical; they have separate and distinctive languages and cultures, and their experiences have been shaped by differing historical circumstances. The disparity between the boarding schools founded by southeastern tribes and the federally run boarding schools to which the children of other tribes were sent is shocking.

The Chickasaw boarding schools are unique in that the tribe founded and sponsored academies, as well as neighborhood day schools, long before the federal government took control of the Chickasaw school system. Of the Chickasaw boarding schools, Bloomfield in particular stands out, chiefly because it was considered significant enough to remain in operation forty years after Oklahoma statehood. This research has special significance for the Chickasaw Nation — especially for the women who attended the academy and their descendants — because it will help to preserve Chickasaw stories and heritage. This book is particularly significant for me — because I wrote it for and with the help of my family.

Values, Purposes, and Community Goals

In this book, I focus on the type of education the students of Bloomfield Academy received and why. When I first began to research the school, I was astounded, by the curriculum, by the pictures, by the attitude of many of the alumnae — largely because of the vast difference between Bloomfield and off-reservation schools I had read about. I became intensely curious. Why was Bloomfield different? In its history as a boarding academy for girls, Bloomfield had three different administrations: mission, tribal, and federal. I noticed that each administration substantially changed the curriculum of the school. Why? To what end? What sort of lives were the students being prepared to lead and why? To participate in what community? White? Tribal? Both? Missionaries, Chickasaws, and federal educators provided literacy training through formal schooling because doing so was valuable and useful, yes, to the Chickasaw girls, but more importantly to themselves, for their own purposes. Each administration had a specific agenda for educating the Chickasaw girls and for educating them in a specific way. My objective is to examine the elements of the curriculum offered at Bloomfield under each administration and the purposes and implications of each — the implications are significant. At its core, this study is a question of identity. The bottom line is that any administration's agenda or objective was really about what identity that administration wanted the students to have: Chickasaw citizen or U.S. citizen? Subservient woman or community leader? It is particularly interesting to me that most of the students who attended Bloomfield were mixed-blood students. I interviewed fifteen women who attended the school, all of whom, like me, are mixed-blood. This study becomes, then, a story of mixed-blood students, mixed literacies, mixed cultures, and mixed identities; Bloomfield is the site where all of these issues intersect and intertwine.

I chose to examine these complicated issues through the lens of literacy and language. This is appropriate because literacy/language is the medium of negotiation, and the missionaries, Chickasaw people, federal educators, and students were constantly negotiating questions of identity, purpose, and power. The Chickasaws were negotiating their place in their present situation and in their future in Indian Territory. This was no easy task. They saw formal literacy training as one way to negotiate their future and preserve their nationhood. Literacy is also an appropriate lens for this study because I focus on a particular site, a school, and "Literacy has always and everywhere been the center of the education enterprise. No matter what else it expects of its schools, a culture insists that students learn to read, write, and speak in the officially sanctioned manner." [22]

Schools have historically been used as places to effect change in large groups of people. Bloomfield's three administrations — the missionaries, the Chickasaw Nation, and the federal government — sought to effect change in the lives of the Chickasaw students, and through them, their families and communities. Each administration saw literacy as something to be desired, something of value. Literacy is, if nothing else, a question of value. Literacy is valued, for perhaps different reasons, by those who teach literacy and those who learn literacy. What value literacy has for either party is dependent upon the community and context in which it is used, for literacy is always tied to purpose; it is something to be used, used for something.

Scholar C. H. Knoblauch contends that literacy is, historically, "a compelling value" and that definitions of literacy are always political, incorporating "the social agendas of the definers, serving the needs of the nonliterate only through the mediation of someone's vision of the way the world should be." The vision of the "definer" then determines the purposes of literacy, directly affecting the curriculum and pedagogies of schools, which are important, formal sites of literacy instruction. Knoblauch goes on to say: "Literacy never stands alone in these perspectives as a neutral denoting of skills; it is always literacy for something . . . for civic responsibility and the preservation of heritage, for personal growth and self-fulfillment, for social and political change."[23]

Knoblauch's contention informs this project in important ways. Bloomfield's three administrations — the missionaries, the Chickasaw Nation, and the federal government — established and changed the literacy curricula offered based on their values and differing purposes of literacy. Each of Bloomfield's administrations had agendas that served two purposes: the betterment of the administration itself and the "betterment" of the Chickasaw students, families, and tribal nation. "Betterment" in this second case means whatever the administration thought was the appropriate sort of life for the Chickasaw women and the people of the Chickasaw Nation, such as subservience or upward mobility. What is especially interesting however, is that during each administration, the literacy "learners," that is the students, families, and Chickasaw people, also had an agenda, the purpose of which was also for their own betterment. Under missionary and federal control, the agendas of the literacy teachers and students competed for fulfillment.

Definitions

The term literacy is complicated. My own definition stems from the "ideological model" of literacy that Brian Street sets forth in Literacy in Theory and Practice. Street constructs a list of the major characteristics of the ideological model of literacy; some of the most salient characteristics are as follows: (1) "the meaning of literacy depends upon the social institutions in which it is embedded"; (2) "literacy can only be known to us in forms which already have political and ideological significance and it cannot, therefore, be helpfully separated from that significance and treated as though it were an 'autonomous' thing"; (3) "the particular practices of reading and writing that are taught in any context depend upon such aspects of social structure as stratification . . . and the role of educational institutions"; (4) "the processes whereby reading and writing are learnt are what construct the meaning of it for particular practitioners"; (5) "we would probably more appropriately refer to 'literacies' than to any single 'literacy.' " [24]

My definition, based on Street's ideological model, directly ties literacy to reading and writing, that is, literacy events and practices, which see orality and literacy as intertwined. However, in this project, literacy goes beyond literacy events and practices to include "related skills." [25] It is particularly important to tie related skills to my definition of literacy because of the context of the study. Each of Bloomfield's administrations had a specific agenda for literacy education. Literacy was seen as the appropriate tool to acculturate the Chickasaws and turn them into efficient and religious U.S. citizens. In order to accomplish this task, the administrations had to include more than reading and writing in their curricula; Bloomfield students had to be introduced to the "hidden curriculum" — the appropriate social skills and cultural conventions, traditions, and ideologies. [26] However, in this case, the desire for Indian students to learn the appropriate social skills, conventions, and ideologies was hardly hidden. Indeed, reformers, missionaries, and policymakers staunchly believed that these related skills were of equal importance — in fact, of even greater importance — than basic reading and writing skills, and they voiced their opinions loudly. [27] As Christian reformer John Oberly contended at the Third Annual Lake Mohonk Conference in 1885,

> To teach an Indian pupil to "read, write and cipher" is not sufficient. He must be taught many things that need not be taught to a white pupil. He must be taught . . . to abandon the religion of his fathers, and accept a new faith; to cast off the social conditions of his own people and receive those of another people . . . he is a twig bent out of perpendicular, and he must be straightened so that the tree will stand erect, inclining no way. . . . In addition to lessons in morals; in religion, in literature, in history. . . . He should be instructed in our theory of government, and in our ideas of property and business. . . . He should be taught how to cultivate the soil after he has been taught how to own it. . . . The Indian boy

pupil should . . . be taught how to build houses . . . make wagons, harness and saddles. . . . And the girl pupil should be instructed in household ways — should be taught how to cook; how to wash and iron clothing; how to handle the needle; how to nurse the sick; how to be a good wife and a good mother.[28]

Clearly, these "related skills" were just as important to the achievement of the purpose of each administration as the more specific literacy subjects and consequently must be included in my definition of literacy because "reading and writing are . . . located within the real social and linguistic practices that give them meaning." [29]

I identify below four major types of literacy curricula or literacy strands offered under each administration, which together form a comprehensive education program in citizenship. Under each administration, one particular literacy strand stands out as the most heavily emphasized, perhaps the most valued, indicating that administration's primary goal or purpose. Bloomfield students received instruction in courses that constitute four major categories: academic, social, religious, and domestic. The categories, or literacy curricula, are defined as follows:

Academic Literacy Curriculum. The first type of curriculum, academic, includes all of the "standard" school classes: reading, writing, arithmetic, history, and so on. Academic literacy includes whatever subject matter society considers "basic" or rudimentary knowledge, knowledge considered necessary to function and participate as an educated person in society. Of all of the categories, academic literacy is the most directly tied to basic reading and writing abilities and the interpretation of text. Every school subject requires the reading of a particular subject matter in textbooks and also the completion of written homework assignments and tests.

Social Literacy Curriculum. Social literacy, the second major type of curriculum, includes training in "extracurricular" subjects, including music and elocution, which are directly tied to basic literacy, but also including other similar and related skills such as art and dancing and proficiency in social traditions and conventions such as etiquette and manners. Art, dancing, and etiquette are related skills considered necessary to be "cultured," "refined," and socially mobile. These related skills are equally as important as music and elocution, even though they are not directly tied to print literacy. Knowledge of social customs and norms is a necessary part of acculturation, the purpose of literacy education for Bloomfield students.

Religious Literacy Curriculum. The third type of curriculum, religious literacy, includes not just actual classes in religion — for example, Sunday school and Bible study — but also training in daily religious rituals, such as attending sermons and devotionals, praying before meals and bedtime, singing hymns, and teaching others the word of God. Religious literacy is tied to reading and writing through the use of the Bible, catechisms, and hymnals and through listening to and interpreting sermons and devotionals, which are usually literacy events. This knowledge is considered necessary for religious conversion and to aid in the conversion of others.

Domestic Literacy Curriculum. Domestic literacy, the final type of curriculum, includes instruction in cooking, sewing, cleaning, gardening, tending animals, child care, and personal hygiene and health, knowledge considered necessary for daily living and homemaking. Home economics instruction in cooking and sewing are directly tied to reading and writing because students use cookbooks and recipes, sewing patterns, and women's fashion magazines. Gardening, cleaning, tending animals, child care, and personal hygiene and health may not always be tied to literacy events but are certainly related skills necessary to proficiency in homemaking, a significant aspect of acculturation.

By placing greater emphasis on one type of curriculum over another, Bloomfield's administrations revealed what they believed to be the purpose of literacy education for the Chickasaw females, that is, what type of lives they believed the students would or should lead. By analyzing the literacy practices at Bloomfield under the three administrations, I examine what the mission and objectives of each administration were and to what extent those objectives were achieved.

Although I could have described or compared the literacy experiences of students at several Indian boarding schools, I chose to look only at the literacy practices of Chickasaw students at Bloomfield because we can more fully realize the power of literacy to manipulate and effect change when we examine how it was used and why in a specific context, for specific community goals. Each administration used literacy to serve a specific agenda; however, Chickasaw people found ways to use literacy education to further their own goals throughout the school's history and to orchestrate their own identities. By encouraging their children to attend mission schools in their Mississippi homeland in the early 1800s, by sending their children to eastern schools while waiting for their academies to be built, by building their own academies in conjunction with missionaries after their forced removal from their homeland, the Chickasaw people proved that they saw literacy education as inherently valuable because it was useful to them, to their purposes. Literacy, for the Chickasaw Nation, was a tool, a weapon used defensively and offensively in the fight for their national survival.

Responsibilities

Research of any kind is a matter of various responsibilities — as an information gatherer, interpreter, analyst, narrator, and scholar. Historical research in particular carries with it certain ethical responsibilities of which I am very aware. This research is traditional in that I do follow an archival model and do attempt to offer a "factual" account of Bloomfield's history; however, I am in no way attempting to offer a "complete" history of the academy. I am not attempting to "correct," "rewrite," or "replace" an already existing story. Rather, this research attempts to add to the history of American Indian education and history of women's literacy education by adding a specific, untold story, by adding a new thread to the stories that already exist. As a historical researcher, I am aware that the writing of histories is inherently ideological; manifested in this book is my own ideological position — that literacy instruction is never a neutral process but is inherently political. I do not suggest that this analysis of Bloomfield is in any way a "complete" or "true" account. The analysis is my interpretation of the information gathered from archival research and interviews. However, it is not my intention to purposefully distort or exaggerate any details, facts, or other information used.

In order to examine the type of literacy practices used at Bloomfield under federal control, from Oklahoma statehood in 1907 to 1949, I chose to turn to the students, for the story of Bloomfield is, after all, their story. I would very much have liked to include the stories of women who attended the academy in its earliest years; unfortunately, I was unable to do so. Very few women who attended the academy before Oklahoma statehood are still living. Furthermore, Bloomfield suffered several fires in its history, and much to my regret, letters, diaries, and other written accounts are difficult to come by. I did have the opportunity to talk with several women who attended the academy between 1911 and 1949 and have included first-person accounts whenever possible. It is important to note, however, that interviewing former students does not make this study an ethnography per se. A true ethnography examines a site that is still in existence or operation. Because Bloomfield integrated with the Ardmore Public School System in 1953, performing a true ethnographic study was impossible; however, listening to the stories of women who attended the academy in its later years was an essential part of this research.

I am very aware as a researcher that interviewing former students and using their stories in my research is a tremendous ethical responsibility. Consequently, I have made a conscious effort not to appropriate the women's voices but to let them speak for themselves to whatever extent possible. However, no research is free from the ideological interpretation of the researcher. I am an acculturated mixed-blood Chickasaw, a university professor, from a family proud of its heritage and interested and active in tribal affairs. The women I interviewed, also mixed-blood, are relatives of mine or friends of relatives. The responsibility I feel to my family and tribe is great. My responsibility and goal as a researcher and scholar have been to understand and respect the researcher-informant relationship as well as to be self-conscious and critical of my own ideological position in order to protect my own integrity, the integrity of this research, and, finally, the integrity of the women who were kind enough to participate in it.

I had the opportunity to listen to fifteen women who attended the academy between 1911 and 1949, several of whom are relatives. This book would not have been possible without the stories of the women I interviewed, all of whom were generous with their time, memories, and personal belongings. The telling of the story is a matter of continuance. The story of Bloomfield Academy is made up of the stories of the people who lived it. Listed below are those who share their stories here, the dates they attended Bloomfield, their tribal affiliation, and their current residence:

>Pauline Williford Adkins
>   Attended from 1932 to 1941
>   Chickasaw, Lebanon, Oklahoma
>
>Fanny Hughes Bass
>   Attended from 1911 to 1914
>   Chickasaw, Tishomingo, Oklahoma
>
>Jeanne Liddell Cochran
>   Attended from 1929 to 1933
>   Chickasaw, Houston, Texas
>
>Clara Pittman Gatlin
>   Attended between 1940 and 1947
>   Choctaw, Durant, Oklahoma
>
>Dorothy Wall Holt
>   Attended from 1940 to 1947
>   Choctaw, Ardmore, Oklahoma

Leona Williford Isaac
Attended from 1933 to 1941
Chickasaw, Oklahoma City, Oklahoma

Claudine Williford King
Attended from 1939 and 1948
Chickasaw, Newkirk, Oklahoma

Hettie McCauley King
Attended between 1925 and 1930
Chickasaw, Ardmore, Oklahoma

Ida Bell Hughes Martin
Attended between 1920 and 1930
Chickasaw, Tishomingo, Oklahoma

Mary Pittman Parris
Attended between 1935 and 1945
Choctaw, Durant, Oklahoma

Frances Griffin Robinson
Attended from 1927 to 1929
Chickasaw, Lebanon, Oklahoma

Fannye Williford Skaggs
Attended from 1939 to 1947
Chickasaw, Moore, Oklahoma

Juanita Keel Tate
Attended in 1918
Chickasaw, Ardmore, Oklahoma

Ula Mae Pittman Welch
Attended between 1940 and 1947
Choctaw, Durant, Oklahoma

Ora Lee Chuculate Woods
Attended from 1930 to 1936
Cherokee, Durant, Oklahoma

2

Chickasha chepota alhehat holisso apisa aiyacha
itanumpoli micha holissochi (Chickasaw Children
Go to School to Read and Write)
Schooling as Tradition

❋

There is no such thing as a *neutral* education process. Education either functions
as an instrument that is used to facilitate the integration of the younger generation into the logic of the present system and bring about conformity to it, *or* it
becomes "the practice of freedom," the means by which men and women deal
critically and creatively with reality and discover how to participate in the transformation of their world. — RICHARD SHAULL, *foreword to* Pedagogy of the
Oppressed *by Paulo Freire*

As I researched American Indian boarding schools, I became increasingly aware of the radical differences between the experiences of students at federally run off-reservation schools and the students at boarding schools founded and operated by the southeastern tribes. I began to
question why the southeastern tribes, and particularly the Chickasaws,
had such markedly different experiences than other tribes. In order to
find answers for my questions, I dug deeper into the Chickasaws' history
to discover what distinctive historical circumstances might have influenced their educational history. I read more and more about the urgency
of the Chickasaws to build schools in Indian Territory. I questioned why
the Chickasaws were so anxious to begin the schooling process. What
prior experiences caused them to see literacy instruction as such a
pressing need? I realized that the unique story of Bloomfield does not

actually begin in 1850 with the building of the school in Indian Territory. In fact, the story begins much, much earlier in Mississippi, the Chickasaws' homeland, when Chickasaw people, fighting for survival, had their first experiences with literacy training. Many Chickasaws did not resist the literacy training provided by missionaries, and unlike members of other tribes during the early 1800s, they welcomed it and then sought it.[1] A look at the early culture of the Chickasaws and the historical circumstances that influenced them may help to explain this reaction.

Early Chickasaw History

The Chickasaws claimed a large territory in what is now northeastern Mississippi, with lands extending east into Alabama and north into western Tennessee and Kentucky. They were a small community of approximately 3,500 to 4,500 members before European contact and were far outnumbered by their neighbors, the Choctaws, who may have had as many as 20,000 members at that time.[2] The Chickasaws and Choctaws, both now part of the so-called Five Civilized Tribes of Oklahoma, are closely related and share an intertwining history. As a matter of fact, many scholars propose that the two were once one tribe. According to historian Muriel Wright, "Chickasaw" is a form of "Chickasha," which is a mnemonic for the Choctaw phrase *chikkih ashachi*, literally translated to mean "they left as a tribe not a very great while ago." The two belong to the Muskhogean linguistic family and, except for minor dialectical differences, share the same language.[3]

The Chickasaws and Choctaws also have similar migration legends. The migration story describes the travels of the Chickasaws from their ancient home in the Far West, protected by a large war dog, to their home east of the Mississippi. The tribe was guided east by a sacred pole, which was carried on each day's march by the tribe's holy men. At night, the men placed the pole upright in the ground. Each morning the mystical pole would be pointing toward the east. This continued until after the tribe crossed the Mississippi River. The story often includes two brothers who argue one morning about which way the pole is leaning; they cannot settle their argument, so they diverge, each taking members of the tribe with him.[4] The Choctaws add a detailed creation story to this migration legend, which describes the Muskogees, Cherokees, Chickasaws, and Choctaws emerging, in that order, out of the great Nanih Waiya mound.[5] That the traditional stories of the Chickasaws and Choctaws account for the presence of the other illustrates their intimate relationship, a relationship that still persists.

The Chickasaws were known as fierce warriors and, in spite of their relatively small population, were never known to have lost a battle.[6] The division of labor was very specific. Women and Indian slaves cared for crops and gathered food; men were "hunters and fighters first and agriculturists only on occasion."[7] Like other North American peoples, the Chickasaws had no written language and relied on the oral tradition to pass down important beliefs, customs, and rituals.[8]

The Chickasaw's first European contact came with the arrival of the Spanish explorer Hernando De Soto and his men in 1540. The narrative of the expedition describes their experiences with the "Chicaza." De Soto commanded the Chickasaws to send him two hundred warriors to carry their supplies. The Chickasaws, insulted and enraged, attacked De Soto and his men.[9] They won this battle and in doing so "made the greatest stroke for freedom in the early history of the Southeast."[10] By this time, the Chickasaws had settled in seven towns in the lower Mississippi valley.[11] Each village consisted of several summer and winter houses. The winter houses were circular, had a pinewood framework, and were covered in plaster and thatched with grass. The rectangular summer houses had clay-plastered walls, which were whitewashed on the outside and inside.[12] The summer house was divided into two rooms, making it a forerunner of the double log cabin.[13]

The Chickasaws organized themselves socially into two major divisions or groups. Each consisted of several clans or groups of blood-related families, matrilineal in descent.[14] Family relationships were extremely important. According to Henry Cushman's early narrative, "every grandson and granddaughter became the grandson and granddaughter of the whole tribe, since all the uncles of a given person were considered as his fathers also; and all the mothers' sisters were mothers; the cousins, as brothers and sisters; the nieces, as daughters; and the nephews as sons."[15] Kinship roles carried with them very specific obligations and duties, particularly in the upbringing of children.

The tribal government played a major role in the social structure of the Chickasaws. Each clan was ruled by a subchief. The head chief, or *mi'ko*, a term often translated as "king," was selected from the highest-ranking clan and served for life. The next-highest-ranking person was the war chief, or *tishu mi'ko*.[16] The *Hopaye*, or Holy Men, were especially significant in the tribal structure, because religion was manifested in every aspect of the Chickasaws social and government organization.[17] They believed in *Ababinili*, a supreme being or spirit that consisted of four elements — the Sun, the Clouds, Clear Sky, and He That Lives in the Clear Sky; *Hottuck Ishtohoollo*, a good spirit or spirits; and *Hottuck Ookproose*, an evil spirit or spirits.[18] Chickasaws believed in life after death and followed an elaborate burial procedure to help the person on the journey to the next life.[19] Like virtually all of the southeastern tribes, the Chickasaw's chief religious ceremony and celebration was the Green Corn Ceremony, held between early spring and late summer.[20] The ceremony, in various forms, is still an important ritual for many southeastern tribes.

By 1700 English traders established trading operations with the Chickasaws, making them British allies until the American Revolution, when they sided with the colonies and even sent men to serve in the colonial armies.[21] The military alliances and trading operations affected the Chickasaw's lifestyle tremendously. This early contact with European culture shaped them culturally, eventually leading to intermarriage, early bilingualism, and further acculturation. The Chickasaws had a long history of adopting captives or people from smaller tribes into their own community;[22] consequently, when white traders married Chickasaw women, tribal leaders invited them to become members of the tribe, participants in their complex family and kinship structures.

In the 1720s and 1730s, several white traders married into the tribe, among them, Logan Colbert, James Gunn, John Gilchrist, Malcomb McGee, James Allen, and John Bynum.[23] The mixed-blood families by these names quickly became some of the most prominent and politically active in the tribe and directly influenced the fate of the Chickasaw Nation.

Some Chickasaws began to mix white customs with their own, appropriating some elements and discarding others. The traders' businesses became Chickasaw businesses, and with the influence of mixed-blood members, many Chickasaws turned to agricultural pursuits. Some rejected any change in traditional lifestyles altogether; others initially resisted but then succumbed to changes; still others found ways to accommodate those changes. It is important to note that the white men who became members of the tribe did just that — they became members. They, too, had to change, and in various ways they rejected, resisted, and accommodated. Members of both cultures influenced each other, all within the boundaries of the Chickasaw communities and family and government systems. Significantly, the mixed-blood men were frequently the members who negotiated with other traders and, most importantly, with the United States government on the Chickasaws' behalf; this would later be the cause of much tension within the tribe. The intermarriage of the Chickasaw women is especially significant because it explains the Chickasaws' early interest in the English language and in literacy training, which was vital to the mixed-blood's business negotiations.

By the end of the eighteenth century, an ever-increasing tide of white settlers pushed further west and saw the Chickasaws and other southeastern tribes as barriers to their progress. They demanded that the federal government solve the "Indian problem" quickly. Consequently, the Chickasaw's official relationship with the United States began in 1786 when the first Chickasaw treaty was signed at Hopewell, South Carolina. The treaty established boundary and trade agreements with the United States.[24] The Chickasaw Nation would sign fourteen treaties with the U.S. government between 1786 and 1902 and two with the

Choctaw Nation.[25] During this time, more and more Chickasaw people turned to agriculture, and many Chickasaws, predominantly mixed-blood families, accumulated much wealth by developing sizable farms, plantations, and livestock herds, and some even invested in slaves.[26]

This was an important time in the history of the Chickasaw Nation because during negotiations with the U.S. government many of the mixed-bloods became increasingly interested in tribal politics and began to take over tribal management from the full-bloods, and because the Chickasaws, preparing for a battle for national survival and working toward continuing economic success, became increasingly interested in the education of their children. For the Chickasaw people, literacy education was neither a neutral process nor a simplistic one. If, as Richard Shaull suggests, education serves to "facilitate the integration of the younger generation into the logic of the present system and bring about conformity to it," then the literacy training of the Chickasaw children would have taught them to become subservient — the only role allowed Indians in the "system" of the 1800s. Many Chickasaws welcomed and encouraged literacy training, not so they could become laborers, but so that they could compete economically. Their goal was to participate equally in the present system, not to overthrow the system, but to redefine their allotted role within that system.

Is this goal the "practice of freedom," as described by Shaull? Was literacy a way for tribal members to "deal critically and creatively with reality and discover how to participate in the transformation of their world?" "Transformation" for the Chickasaws was a complicated issue. Their culture, their entire way of life, was being "transformed" by the white culture whether they liked it or not. The Chickasaws were unable to fight for their old ways of life and may or may not have wanted to. Were they trying to "participate in the transformation of their world?" Perhaps what they were attempting through literacy was to participate in how their world was transformed and to gain a measure a control over their way of life in the new system. Literacy was a way to provide that control.

Religious Literacy Instruction in Mississippi

The Chickasaws' desire for literacy training led to their first contact with missionaries who worked to integrate them into a major facet of the "present system," Christianity. The New York Presbyterian missionary society sent the first missionary to the Chickasaws, Reverend Joseph Bullen, in 1799. Bullen wisely decided not to establish either a church or a school in the nation but instead elected to visit people in their homes, teaching them to write their names. Using an interpreter, he shared the biblical stories of creation, the flood, and other events, stories that resonated with Chickasaws perhaps because the stories seemed very similar to their own. On these visits he brought along his young son, who taught Chickasaw children how to read and write. Bullen, though treated well by Chickasaw families, left the nation in 1803.[27]

No missionaries visited the Chickasaws again until 1819, when the Presbyterian, Methodist, and Baptist churches sent representatives as a direct result of new federal policy. In 1810, Congress created the American Board of Commissioners for Foreign Missionaries (ABCFM) and in 1819 passed the Indian Civilization Fund Act, legislation that invited Protestant missionaries to establish Indian schools and allowed them to offer religious education if they would also include secular subjects. The Civilization Fund, an annual appropriation of $10,000, was administered by the superintendent of Indian Affairs for this purpose, and the missionary societies received grants from the government to support their endeavors.[28] This legislation is particularly significant because it indicates that literacy training was capable of "civilizing" tribes. Civilization meant acculturation, which entailed more than learning to read and write; acculturation included learning the appropriate ideologies, cultural conventions, traditions, and social skills. Policymakers wanted the Indians "civilized." Evangelical Protestant missionary groups wanted the Indians "Christianized." That the government chose to ally themselves with Protestant missionaries and even appropriate funds, thereby forming a direct partnership between church and state, underscores the pervasive national belief that Christianity, civilization, and American citizenship were inextricably intertwined. Both parties probably considered the education arrangement a fair trade. Chickasaws, satisfied with their own religious system, were generally not interested in religious literacy training; however, many members, particularly those from mixed-blood families, were hungry for basic academic literacy training and took advantage of what was provided. Although the federal government would not begin to establish and operate its own boarding schools until the latter part of the nineteenth century, the Indian Civilization Fund marked the beginning of what educational historians call "colonial education" for American Indians, that is, education designed to acculturate the Indians and at the same time engender subservience and perpetuate inequality.[29]

The South Carolina–Georgia Synod and the Cumberland Presbyterian Association, which established mission schools in the early 1820s, made the most significant educational effort in the Chickasaw community before the Chickasaw removal. The Cumberland Presbyterian Association founded Charity Hall in 1820, and in 1822, the South Carolina-Georgia Synod established Monroe School for Chickasaw children between the ages of six and sixteen.[30] The most successful of these schools was Monroe, which was located near the Natchez Trace and the Chickasaw Agency. The school received federal aid for Indian student tuition in the amount of $500 to $800 annually and enrolled approximately fifty to eighty students. In the school's early years, the majority of its students were from mixed-blood families; however, as the Chickasaw community became more comfortable with the school system, the full-blood population increased. Monroe began as a day school, but after a year of operation it became a boarding school so that students throughout the Chickasaw nation could attend. Students learned to farm on the school's one-hundred-acre demonstration farm and produced most of the food needed to run the boarding school themselves.[31]

The boarding school–demonstration farm model used in the 1820s was a forerunner of the "manual labor academy," an educational model that experienced only brief popularity in the United States in the mid-1800s. Manual labor academies were based on the concept of Swiss aristocrat Phillip von Fellenberg's schools in Hofwyl, Switzerland. Von Fellenberg believed that schools should educate and socialize and, accordingly, that the children of poor families should be socialized to be satisfied with their places in life. American educator Joseph Cogswell, who had visited the Hofwyl school in 1818, imported the idea because manual labor academies were cost-efficient and because students could learn trades. Their fall from popularity was due to the fact that many families wanted their children to attend school so that they would not have to be farmers and mechanics.[32] However, if manual labor or industrial model schools were not thought appropriate for white children, they were deemed entirely appropriate for women, African Americans, and American Indians and are classified as colonial schools today. By the 1880s, the federally operated reservation and off-reservation boarding schools, schools that too many children were forced to attend, were based on the manual labor plan.[33]

Chickasaws, however, in spite of the colonial model on which the school was based, found the boarding school–demonstration farm model at Monroe very effective, chiefly because many families were becoming comparatively wealthy landowners, and agriculture was a significant part of the economic base of the entire nation. In fact, Chickasaw leaders demonstrated their satisfaction with the educational system by appropriating $5,000 from tribal funds to build more schools and another $2,500 per year for expenses in 1824, just two years after Monroe was founded. Tribal appropriations far exceeded the federal aid missionaries were receiving from the Civilization Fund, which had a total operating budget of $10,000 a year. The additional schools were Tokshish, Martyn, and Caney Creek. Tokshish School, which was established in 1824, had a small farm but operated as a day school instead of a boarding school and enrolled approximately twenty students. Martyn School, which had a large demonstration farm, was established at Pigeon Roost as a boarding school in 1825 with an enrollment of about thirty students. Caney Creek School, also a boarding school, was established in 1826 in western Alabama, forty miles from the nearest Chickasaw town. Missionaries established Caney Creek at this location purposely so children would be far from their families and traditional way of life — a way of life seen as "barbarous" by missionaries.[34] This same motive would also drive the federal government and Protestant reformers to favor "off-reservation" boarding schools rather than reservation boarding schools or day schools and to force attendance.[35]

The course of study at the Monroe, Tokshish, Martyn, and Caney Creek Schools consisted of three types of literacy curricula: religious, domestic, and academic. The objective of the school was "to train the head, heart, and hand" of Chickasaw children in order to improve their lives in this world and to prepare them for one in heaven. The academic literacy curriculum or "head" studies, in addition to basic English literacy, included spelling, English grammar, written composition, geography, and arithmetic, subjects that are directly tied to basic reading and writing abilities. The domestic literacy curriculum was based on a specific societal division of labor, and girls were instructed in "hand" activities such as sewing, weaving, and other homemaking skills, skills tied to basic reading and writing through the use of patterns and recipes. The boys' domestic literacy curriculum included agriculture, carpentry, and blacksmithing, subjects that may have been tied to basic reading and writing through the use of almanacs, catalogs, measurements, or bookkeeping.[36] All students were given training for the "heart" or religious literacy training based on the bible.

The major problems the missionaries faced were a shortage of teachers, the language barrier, and the Chickasaws' general lack of interest in religious training. The missionaries solved their staffing problem by turning to the monitorial or Lancastrian method of school, in which older students taught or monitored the younger ones.[37] This model, developed in the early 1800s by Joseph Lancaster, was very popular at poorer institutions.[38] The language barrier was not as easy to overcome. In order to facilitate the English literacy process, missionaries experimented with boarding some Caney Creek students at the homes of white settlers who lived near the nation. This method was considered fairly successful. Although instruction was primarily in English, missionaries occasionally used the Chickasaws' slaves as interpreters and quickly established a good working relationship with them. The slaves found the idea of salvation much more attractive than tribal members and quickly populated the mission's church pews.[39] In general, Chickasaws were not interested in converting to Christianity, and missionaries had great difficulty overcoming this third obstacle.

The Chickasaw people were interested in literacy training because of the changing population of their community and family structures and because they saw it as essential to their continuing economic success and success in U.S. negotiations. They had invested in the schools themselves and were annoyed by the amount of school time missionaries devoted to the religious literacy. The tribal council's largest complaint was that there was more religious literacy training going on than the secular training they desired. Anson Gleason, a missionary teacher at Tokshish, observed that "The great outcry against the missionaries has been, that they were not teaching school, which, it was said, was their appropriate work; and that, if we kept on this way, we should get the people all crazy and spoiled, like the Choctaws."[40] His comment indicates that the Chickasaws cared very much about what kind of literacy training their children received. That the Chickasaws described teaching school as the "appropriate work" of the missionaries demonstrates that the Chickasaws believed that the purpose of schooling was academic, not religious. Furthermore, the Chickasaws apparently believed that not only was religious literacy training inappropriate, but it could even be harmful, causing the people to become "crazy and spoiled" like their longtime neighbors and rivals, the Choctaws.

Although both the missionaries and the Chickasaw people were interested in the establishment and continuing operation of the schools, tribal and missionary literacy goals conflicted. The Chickasaws, knowing that both the white settlers in the region and the federal government wanted them out of the way at any cost, needed academic literacy skills to successfully negotiate with the government and to compete economically, giving them leverage in negotiations. The missionaries were not interested in providing the Chickasaws with solid academic training. They were interested only in making the Chickasaws functionally literate, that is, able to read and write well enough to participate in church services, study the Bible, and be converted to Christianity.

In spite of the conflicting goals of the missionaries and the Chickasaws, missionary schools served an important purpose for both parties, and both the Chickasaws and the missionaries eventually achieved their literacy goals. For as historian Muriel Wright points out, although "the work and influence of mission churches . . . were never predominant in the nation . . . all the Chickasaw are Christianized and the majority are church members today." [41] At the same time, many graduates of Monroe and the other mission schools became tribal business and political leaders for the nation, thus achieving tribal literacy goals.[42]

Removal to Indian Territory and National Rebuilding

The history of the Chickasaw mission schools in Mississippi was short-lived. Forced removal, the Chickasaw people's greatest fear, had become reality. White settlers demanded Indian land — indeed, they were already encroaching upon it — and in yet another attempt to solve the "Indian problem," Congress passed the Indian Removal Act in 1830 under the pressure of President Andrew Jackson. The Removal Act authorized the federal government to negotiate with tribes for the exchange of their land and stipulated that the relocated tribes would be provided with removal costs and subsistence for one year after their relocation.[43] For the people of the Chickasaw Nation, the consequences of this act were dramatic. For years, the federal government had voiced their intentions to "civilize" Indians so that they could become American citizens and live in harmony with whites in the United States. They told Indian tribes to speak English, to become Christian, to educate their children, to farm. Ironically, although Chickasaws were learning to speak English, becoming Christianized, educating their children, and farming — to such an extent that they were, in fact, named one of the Five "Civilized" Tribes, federal government officials and white settlers wanted them out of the way, wanted them *removed*, and found a way to force Indian nations to comply. The passage of the Removal Act indicates a belief that Indians could become "Americanized" or "Civilized" but could never have equal status. In the words of Lawrence Cremin, "the prevailing assumption was clear: people could be educated to transcend the barriers of ethnicity and religion in order to become full-fledged members of the American community, but they could not be educated to transcend the barriers of race." [44]

What U.S. policymakers had not counted on was the ability of Indian nations to adopt white ways without losing their own tribal identities. The Chickasaw Nation, by this time, had accumulated substantial wealth. Chickasaws still lived on their ancient homeland and, in addition, owned millions of acres of land, farms, and plantations. Their children attended Chickasaw schools. They had developed a uniquely Chickasaw form of government. They conducted business as the Chickasaw Nation and had national funds. They were mixing new ways with traditional ways, and they were doing so *as a nation*. On the eve of removal, the Chickasaws enjoyed an amazing degree of autonomy and independence, and in spite of the internal conflict every culture experiences and the significant external challenges they faced, they maintained and even strengthened their deep-seated national identity. The passage of the Removal Act was a crushing blow.

The Chickasaw leaders, who had become shrewd businessmen, began negotiating with the government and used a number of means to delay their removal. This was a time of tremendous internal conflict and anxiety: removal was imminent, some sort of deal had to be struck, all members worried about whether or not their interests would be protected, and tension between mixed-blood members and full-blood members heightened. [45] The Chickasaws' morale and spirit plummeted. They could not imagine their future in Indian Territory, and their present was quickly becoming unbearable. Chickasaws knew the fate of the other southeastern tribes that had already begun the Trail of Tears. White settlers and whiskey traders flooded onto their land, and the state governments of Mississippi and Alabama adopted laws to nullify the Chickasaw Nation's powers and made provisions to punish any violators; the U. S. government deliberately offered no protection. [46] In their treaties with the federal government, Chickasaw leaders expressed their attachment to their homeland by writing, "The Chickasaws are about to abandon their homes, which they have long cherished and loved"; but, nevertheless, they demonstrated their determination to do whatever was necessary to preserve their sovereignty and independence. In the Treaty of 1834, they wrote: "The Chickasaw Nation find themselves oppressed in their present situation by being made subject to the laws of the States in which they reside. . . . Rather than submit to this great evil, they prefer to seek a home in the West, where they may live and be governed by their own laws."[47]

Finally, in 1837, the Chickasaws and Choctaws signed the Treaty of Doaksville, which provided for the settlement of the Chickasaws in the Choctaw Nation in Indian Territory.[48] The terms of the treaty mandated that the Chickasaws "were to have equal representation in the Choctaw General Council with the citizens of other districts organized under the Choctaw (q.v.) government." If further stipulated that "all financial affairs of the two nations should be kept entirely separate and under the control of their respective officers," a condition necessary for the Chickasaws to retain their status as a separate nation.[49] The early literacy training of the Chickasaws served them well in their negotiations, and they "fared better than all other tribes."[50] They used the literacy the federal government had wanted them to attain in order to delay their own removal, maintain their sovereignty, and protect the economic welfare of their members.

Amazingly, on the eve of their own removal, as they closed down their schools, Chickasaw leaders made arrangements for some children to attend the Choctaw Academy in Blue Springs, Kentucky, which was established in 1825. One child, the son of Chickasaw chief Levi Colbert, was sent as early as 1828. Between 1834 and 1839, the years of removal, over sixty Chickasaw boys were enrolled at various times in the Choctaw Academy.[51] Chickasaw leaders and families knew that the coming years would be extraordinarily hard, and they could not predict the fate of the people. By sending these boys to school in Kentucky, Chickasaw leaders and families spared them, to some extent, the trauma of removal and, at the same time, ensured a better future for the Chickasaw Nation, as well as for the boys themselves. Making arrangements to continue the literacy education of some of their children was an act of incredible foresight and optimism.

By 1837, Chickasaw leaders could no longer delay emigration. The Chickasaws were "the wealthiest of any of the Indian nations" before their removal.[52] No amount of wealth, however, could protect the Chickasaws from sickness and death, hallmarks of the Trail of Tears. Fever, dysentery, and smallpox swept through their membership; more than five hundred Chickasaws died during their removal.[53] When the Chickasaws arrived in Indian Territory, grieving and sick, they found the subsistence supplies promised by the federal government spoiled and inedible, and they had to battle starvation. This problem occurred because of a lack of coordination between the collection of the subsistence supplies and the arrival of the Chickasaws. Officials collected supplies far too early, so that by the time the Chickasaws arrived the provisions were ruined.[54] Private contractors, hired to assist with rationing, took full advantage of the situation, and the Chickasaws did not have the means or spirit to fight the corruption and fraudulence inflicted on them.[55] Starvation, corruption, and demoralization were not the only challenges the Chickasaws confronted in the place that was to be their new home. They were constantly threatened not only by marauding bands of Kiowas, Comanches, and Kickapoos but also by members of the Texas militia in pursuit of these tribes, and Chickasaw people were essentially defenseless on the frontier.[56]

The devastating effects of removal on the Chickasaw people cannot be overstated. They were forced to leave their homes and homeland and to live in a place that they had never seen and could not imagine. Removal affected every aspect of the Chickasaws' already changing way of life — their language, religion, ceremonies, clan systems, government, and livelihood. They had no sense of physical safety or emotional security and no reason to believe that their new home would not be also be taken away. Furthermore, they refused to rebuild their nation while living in the Choctaw district. If the Choctaws somehow gained control of their finances, the Chickasaws could lose their name and status as a nation altogether. Unfortunately, this very nearly happened, and the struggle to maintain control was fierce. According to Muriel Wright, the battle for control "led to feuds among the Chickasaw that . . . resulted in lawlessness and . . . murders." [57]

It was not until 1848, eleven years after removal, that Chickasaws finally settled their economic disputes, writing their first formal constitution and electing Edmund Pickens as chief of the nation. [58] This marked the beginning of a period of national rebuilding, and in 1855, Chickasaw leaders signed one of their most significant treaties. The Treaty of 1855 with the Choctaw Nation defined the legal boundaries of the Chickasaw Nation and gave it "the unrestricted right of self-government and full jurisdiction, over persons and property." [59] The new Chickasaw government immediately redrafted the constitution and laws and established a capitol at Tishomingo. During this time period, the Chickasaw Nation had nearly been subsumed by the Choctaw Nation, but Chickasaw people who had been removed, starved, cheated, and raided refused to lose this final battle — the battle for their name and identity as a people. Chickasaws began farming, opened businesses, and established two newspapers, the *Chickasaw Intelligencer* and the *Chickasaw and Choctaw Heralder*. [60]

Because they knew that education was crucial to their economic success and ultimately to their survival, Chickasaws urgently desired to continue the education of their children and made appropriations for a tribal academy, the Chickasaw Manual Labor Academy for boys, in their first written laws in 1844. They soon opened four other boarding schools for both males and females: the Wapanucka Institute for Girls, 1852; the Bloomfield Academy for Chickasaw Females, 1852; Collins Institute (referred to as Colbert), 1854; and the Burney Institute for Girls, 1859. [61] The use of written laws to appropriate funds for a tribal academy is an especially significant literacy event because it is, in effect, literacy in action — the use of literacy to perpetuate literacy. Using written laws, in English, to make provisions for an academy is an excellent example of the way in which Chickasaw people used literacy, taught to them by whites in order to colonize them, to participate in and gain control over their current situation.

While the academies were under construction, Chickasaw leaders again decided to provide for the education of at least some of their children. Consequently, during the late 1840s, tribal leaders arranged to send approximately fifteen of their young men, predominantly mixed-bloods, to the Delaware College in Newark, Delaware, and the Plainsfield Academy near Norwich, Connecticut. Several of the young men had previously attended the Choctaw Academy in Kentucky. Reports of the boys' progress at school indicate that they received academic, social, and religious literacy training and that they were well received at the school.[62] It is interesting to note, however, that in spite of the length of time some of the students had been away from home, their letters demonstrate a great desire to know the state of affairs at home and to achieve the literacy goals set for them by the Chickasaws. One letter reads:

> We are all well and trying to learn as much as we can. And I care [sic] say, that am very interested to get an Education as well as my people wants me learned, We the boys heard from home and learned that Chickasaw Delegation will be on to washington City. Sometime in November of this inst, Ane we Desired very much for them to go round & see us. in particularly Edmund Pickens, who is one of the delegate, & principal Chief of the nation. You will please & so kind as to advise them to come & see us? . . . Nothing more, at present, But remain your Respectfully and most Humble servant.[63]

The letter indicates that the student wanted to do well in order to please his "people." The use of the term "people" is significant because it demonstrates that he thinks of himself as a member of a nation and that he has a responsibility to that nation. His desire to see members of the Chickasaw delegation attest to his attachment to home and his interest in the goings on of the nation. Unfortunately, not all of the young men sent east returned to Indian Territory. Six of the Chickasaw boys died at Plainsfield, most from tuberculosis.[64]

The fact that Chickasaws sent some children to eastern boarding schools during what must have been a terribly difficult time for them shows how determined they were for their children to continue their literacy education. In a single generation the Chickasaw people had not only persevered through prejudice and hatred, forced removal, sickness, death, and enormous financial loss but had also battled to preserve their identity as a nation. They began constructing schools for their children, but some Chickasaws felt waiting even a few years seemed too long. Now, the Chickasaws' mission was to reconstruct their nation, build leadership, and develop economic enterprises that would ensure their survival and success in Indian Territory. Once again, the Chickasaw people needed tools for transformation. Education was the key.

For Chickasaw people, literacy education was not the "practice of freedom" Shaull suggested in the foreword of Paulo Freire's *Pedagogy of the Oppressed*. For years, the federal government tried to kill Indians or acculturate them. Missionaries tried to civilize and convert them. The Chickasaws fiercely struggled for survival in a world whose goal was to transform their culture by assimilating them and teaching them subservience. The Chickasaw people chose survival, knowing that survival meant change. They were forced to leave Mississippi and move to Indian Territory; removal was inescapable. But the Chickasaws took control of their situation as much as they could, making provisions for their own boarding academies and sending their children to the Choctaw Academy, Delaware College, and Plainsfield Academy a full twenty years before the first federally run off-reservation boarding school opened.

Literacy, for the Chickasaws, was a way to control their own transformation; it was not a practice of freedom but a practice of control — a way to create an acceptable place for themselves in a different world. What government officials and missionaries did not understand was the ability of tribal members to accept "American" ways without rejecting their own culture. The Chickasaws were not passive recipients of literacy and the cultural practices tied to it. As Brian Street discusses in *Social Literacies*, indigenous peoples "find pragmatic ways of adopting elements of the new ideology, or of the new forms in which literacy is introduced, to indigenous belief and practice."[65] This was true for the Chickasaws. Change did not mean the end of tribalism, but tribal preservation. Bloomfield's story began, not in Indian Territory, but in Mississippi when the tribe received their first literacy instruction, thus beginning their long tradition of placing value on education. This early story shows the perseverance and determination of the Chickasaws to school their children and, in doing so, preserve their nation.

3
Chickasha eho himita iholisso apisa
(Chickasaw Girls' School)
Bloomfield under Missionary and Tribal Control
✸

We were taught to *Obey* and everything moved like clock work. The girls all worked and enjoyed it. Right there we learned many lessons that will be with us always. The one above all was to love our neighbor, and from the spirit I see manifested here to-day among you, my little sisters, I feel that that has been the motto of Bloomfield.
— MRS. MEAD, *student of Bloomfield,* 1857

Have it said that you are from Bloomfield. — E. B. HINSHAW,
superintendent of Bloomfield, 1895–1906

Although I grew up in Ardmore, Oklahoma, only a few blocks from Carter Seminary and had classmates who boarded there, I did not realize until I was in college that Carter was once Bloomfield, the school my grandmother attended. I began to ask questions and was amazed at the answers. Claudine went there? It burned how many times? The Chickasaws actually controlled it? My family and I began digging through records at the Chickasaw Council House Museum and local libraries and calling relatives. I kept going, sifting through programs of commencements that occurred a century ago, looking at dozens of photographs of white-gowned young girls as stiff as wedding cake brides, regarding their earnest faces and imagining. What would they say to me now? People gave me more recent programs, pictures, Polly in a Pilgrim dress. What happened there? Questions, questions, questions. Bloomfield was the only one of the Chickasaw schools that remained open

after statehood — until 1949. Why? What happened in the early years
that made it special? What would those people in the pictures say —
what did they say? "Right there we learned many lessons that will
be with us always. The one above all was to love our neighbor." A
Mrs. Mead said that. She started school at Bloomfield in 1857; she was
eight years old. It was run by the missionaries then. "Have it said that
you are from Bloomfield." That was in Nettie Burris's class notes.
Elihu B. Hinshaw was the lecturer. Those were the years of Chickasaw
control — the golden years.

Finding information about the early years of Bloomfield was difficult;
few records remain. Women who attended after Oklahoma statehood
often told me that it was considered a privilege to be a Bloomfield student or that their mothers, sisters, or cousins had gone there, and they
wanted to go, too. Somehow, receiving an education at Bloomfield had
become a tradition. Something was accomplished in the early years of
missionary and tribal control that was obviously very special. The missionaries and the Chickasaws both had visions of what they would accomplish at the school. Literacy, after all, is never without purpose.
What were the purposes of the missionaries and the Chickasaws, and
how did the literacy curricula of the school change to fulfill those goals?

The Mission Years

For the Chickasaw Nation, providing literacy instruction for their children was a matter of survival. After their removal to Indian Territory,
the Chickasaws fought to regain control of their finances and their nation and took every step possible to rebuild their economic base. Knowing that economic success was directly tied to the literacy education of
their children, Chickasaw leaders made provisions to build neighborhood day schools and boarding academies for their children, daughters
as well as sons. Literacy education would help them gain control of
their situation and ensure their future survival and success. Chickasaws,
not quite back on their feet, were not yet able to run the schools themselves. Help was close at hand.

Protestant missionary groups had been working closely with government officials in an effort to solve the "Indian problem" throughout the seventeenth and eighteenth centuries, an alliance that had become even stronger since the Civilization Act of 1819. The missionaries' purposes were obvious. They sincerely wanted to bestow upon the Indians all of the "blessings of civilization," that is, the English language, Christianity, and other necessary "civilized habits." Chickasaws and missionaries had successfully worked together to establish and operate Monroe, Charity Hall, and the other schools in Mississippi, and Chickasaw leaders were not entirely averse to renewing that partnership. Consequently, various Protestant denominations helped the Chickasaws establish their schools. Reverend John Harpole Carr of the Methodist Episcopal Church was selected by the Indian Mission Conference to superintend one of two Chickasaw missionary boarding schools for girls, the Bloomfield Academy.[1]

Before statehood, no organized system of schooling existed; a school was usually only as good as its superintendent. Consequently, Reverend Carr, who remained superintendent of Bloomfield until the Civil War, played a major role in shaping the school and its early traditions, beginning with the actual building of the school. As the story goes, Carr pitched a tent on the selected site, a field of wildflowers, and began construction. The school was originally located near what is now Kemp, Oklahoma, in Bryan County, which was just across the Red River from Denison, Texas, the closest town and principal trade center. In Mississippi, the Chickasaw Nation had supplied the majority of the funds necessary to run their schools, and they continued this tradition in Indian Territory by contributing two-thirds of the funds for Bloomfield's operation, a fact that illustrates their determination to exercise their national autonomy and control the literacy education of their children. The missionary board supplied the remaining one-third.[2]

In addition, the school received $1,000 from the interest earned by money given to George Washington by the first U.S. Congress for his services in the Revolutionary War, which he placed in an education fund, and because of this, the school was nearly named after George

Washington. This would never happen. After former Chickasaw chief Jackson Kemp mailed a letter to Carr in his tent on the flower-covered prairie addressed to "Bloomfield," the school was never called by any other name.[3] Appropriately, the school, founded by the Chickasaw Nation, was named by a Chickasaw.

Reverend Carr, who was a trained carpenter, not only built the school himself but also raised all the food necessary to supply it, planting orchards of apples, peaches, and plums and growing wheat, corn, and potatoes. Although the Chickasaw Nation appropriated two-thirds of Bloomfield's funds, the missionary board appointed the superintendent and had control of the school's operation. Carr received a salary of $600 per year, and teachers received $100, a sum that increased to $250 by the Civil War. The school's budget made appropriations for $66 per pupil annually.[4] At this time, hired help attended to the upkeep of the school; later in the school's history, students did most of the general maintenance.

The missionary board primarily recruited its teachers from New England colleges and academies. In 1852, John Carr married his second wife, Angelina Hosmer, from Bedford, Massachusetts, who was working in the Choctaw mission schools. A graduate of Mount Holyoke, Angelina planned the school's curriculum and schedule. Carr, knowing they would need more help, traveled with his wife to New England, where they recruited Susan (Sarah) J. Johnson of Lenox, Massachusetts. John Carr as superintendent, Angelina Hosmer Carr as matron, and Sarah Johnson as teacher constituted the first staff at Bloomfield when it opened in 1852.[5] The school had only a few other teachers under the Carr administration, all of whom were women.

The mission boards purposely recruited women teachers and believed that they were the perfect choice for Indian school service. Because they had no other employment options, women would provide a "stable, inexpensive teaching force." Furthermore, the conceptualization of women as "Republican Mothers" and symbols of Christian charity was deepening. The proper role of Republican Mothers was to nurture their sons, who were future citizens of the republic, and raise them to be moral and upright republican leaders; the idea of women teachers seemed a natural extension of this role.[6] Women not only could help in the running of the mission schools by cooking, sewing, nursing, and housekeeping but at the same time could serve as pious, Christian role models and "provide a benevolent influence and a refined atmosphere."[7]

Most missionary teachers were young women from the northeastern region of the United States and were graduates of women's academies or colleges like Mount Holyoke, institutions that played a significant role in increasing women's literacy and opportunities.[8] Missionary teaching widened the scope of what women could do in the nineteenth century and, for these women, provided choice where once there had been none.

Teaching at the mission schools was decidedly not a job for the weak in spirit. The work required hard physical labor, and little time was available to rest. Women missionaries taught classes, organized religious services, cooked, cleaned, gardened, and nursed. Emotionally, women had to cope with the homesickness and loneliness that accompany isolation. Many suffered from exhaustion and physical breakdowns. Illnesses plagued the women. According to historian Susan Peterson,

> The most prevalent diseases were bilious fever, pleurisy, consumption, dysentary, whooping cough, scrafula, scurvy, liver trouble, and pneumonia. There were outbreaks of typhoid, measles, cholera, and smallpox to contend with, and many new teachers became weakened from malaria attacks. Some succeeded in regaining their strength during summer vacations, but others did not. . . . Missionary reports to the Commissioner of Indian Affairs contained frequent mention of wives, daughters, or female teachers who died during service in the field.[9]

Angelina Hosmer Carr ranked among these women who lost their lives in Indian Territory; she died in 1864. Both teachers and students experienced severe health problems, and there were "eighteen funerals in that thinly settled neighborhood during that first winter."[10]

Because the school was not finished by December 1852, a neighborhood school was established for both boys and girls until the construction of Bloomfield was completed. Many Chickasaws, anxious to continue their literacy training, sent their children to the neighborhood school while they waited. Sarah Johnson, who married John Carr after Angelina's death and became Sarah Carr, recalls the names of three male students who attended the neighborhood school: Simon Kemp, Martin Allen, and Levi Colbert. These students were the sons of mixed-blood tribal leaders, and their attendance demonstrates the desire of the Chickasaw leaders to educate their own children, serving as role models for other families and influencing Chickasaws' opinions and attitudes about literacy instruction. The school opened its doors in the fall of 1853 to a total of twenty-five students, filling every available seat.[11] Again the Chickasaw leaders proved their support of literacy education as well as their influence over other families. Carr names and describes some of Bloomfield's first students in the following list:

Serena and Lorena Factor, twins, daughters of full blooded indians.

Rebecca Burney, daughter of a deacon of the Cumberland Presbyterian Church.

Rebecca Colbert, sister of Frank Colbert who built the bridge across Red River.

Amelia and Lucy Kemp, daughters of Jackson Kemp.

Mary and Frances Kemp, daughters of Joel Kemp, who owned the ferry.

Mary Ann Colbert, daughter of Morgan Colbert, deacon in Cumberland Presbyterian Church.

Alice Warner, daughter of Dr. Warner. She married Captain Welch, of the Confederate Army.

Mary Reynolds, whose parents resided in the neighborhood.

Elvirn and Elzira Colbert, daughters of Lemuel Colbert and Carter Elzira Hoyt.

Others were: Emily Allen, Sallie Shecho and Mildred Fletcher.[12]

Both the number of students enrolled and the listing of students in-dicates the support the school received from the Chickasaw community. The school's capacity enrollment when it first opened shows the num-ber of families willing to do without their daughters' help at home. Several of these families moved to the area surrounding the academy, which contributed to the growth of Kemp as a town.[13] Carr's list of students shows a number of Kemps and Colberts, families who were among the most active and influential in the governing of the nation. Many of these families were mixed-blood; this may indicate tension be-tween mixed-blood and full-blood Chickasaws or reluctance on the part of full-blood families to educate their children. To offset this tendency, neighborhood schools were frequently established in areas with a high full-blood population to encourage the education of full-blood chil-dren.[14] The education of full-blood children was particularly significant; as full-blood members received more education, they played a much stronger role in the leadership of the nation than they had in earlier years and more fully participated in government, business, and other affairs of the nation.[15]

The missionaries' goal was to "Civilize and Christianize" the Chicka-saws. They chose literacy instruction through formal schooling as the instrument to achieve this goal because they believed in the ideology of literacy. For the missionaries, literacy was the agent of salvation, na-tionalism, individualism, prosperity — every progressive ideal. Literacy and civilization came hand in hand because Christianity could not be achieved without literacy, and the missionaries knew, certainly, that there was no such thing as a "civilized" person who was not a Christian. As Lawrence Cremin contends, "the tie that had existed in the minds of the colonial missionaries between piety and civility, between the ways of Christian belief and the ways of Anglo-American civilization, per-sisted into the national era."[16] Mount Holyoke graduate Angelina Carr established a curriculum at Bloomfield that would help realize the mis-sion's goals: literacy to "Christianize" and "civilize."

The literacy curriculum at Bloomfield under missionary control was

similar to the curriculum of academies for white children that prolifer-
ated during that time. The academy, a uniquely American model of
schooling, constituted the most important type of secondary school in
America during the 1800s, its popularity declining with the rise of the
high school at the end of the 1800s.[17] Academies, sometimes called
seminaries or institutes, were secondary schools that were privately
controlled and financed by individuals or church denominations; however, in most cases, any student who could pay tuition could attend.[18]
Academies were not usually college preparatory schools and differed
substantially from the Latin grammar school model widespread in the
early republic. The classical literacy tradition heavily influenced the curriculum at Latin grammar schools in colonial America, and the all-male
students were likely to have been taught, in addition to Latin grammar,
Cato, Erasmus, Ovid, and Aesop, a curriculum that had outlived its
practicality.[19]

The academy was seen as the answer to the outdated Latin grammar
school model of education; its primary purpose was to teach "ideas and
skills directly related to the practical side of life" and to "provide social
mobility for the average citizen."[20] Some appropriate subjects included
the English language, history, geography, writing, logic and rhetoric,
arithmetic and algebra, and natural and mechanical science.[21] Academies, designed for practicality, were distinctly American and fostered a
nationalistic and frequently evangelical spirit.[22] Literally hundreds of
academies were established in the 1800s. Mount Holyoke and other colleges and seminaries for women were founded and became very well
respected and influential during this period.

The literacy curriculum at the Bloomfield academy had academic,
social, domestic, and religious strands. The daily schedule at Bloomfield was patterned after Mount Holyoke's; morning classes began at
8:30 A.M. and continued with a recess until 12:30 P.M. The academic
literacy curriculum consisted of the following subjects: "if necessary the
English language and the alphabet, spelling, reading, writing and arithmetic, both mental and written, and, as they advanced, natural philoso-

phy, grammar, 'Watts on the Mind,' botany and history of the United States during the regular school hours."[23]

The academic literacy curriculum was patterned after the classical model at Mount Holyoke; however, it is important to note that during this period many of the students enrolled probably had not have received any prior literacy training. The classes offered were primary-level reading and writing courses designed to introduce the students to English literacy, and one of the major problems missionary teachers faced was the language barrier. Some schools tried interpreters, whereas others expected students to learn English as they were taught to read. Neither system was very considered successful.[24] Other academic courses were offered but were probably taught at a primary level as well. At this time, no entrance requirements based on literacy existed, as they did in later years.

Afternoons were devoted to social literacy instruction. According to Carr's narrative, the girls were taught "needle, wax, worsted and coral work, also drawing, painting and vocal music. In each of these departments they showed taste and made fair proficiency." Although learning social skills was an important part of the acculturation or "civilization" process, domestic literacy skills were an even more basic staple, and domestic literacy instruction was a significant feature of Bloomfield. The pupils were also taught "to cut, make and mend their own clothes" in the afternoon, as well as how to do "all the ordinary house work, cooking excepted. The older pupils were taught each Saturday in the pastry department."[25] Older students were expected to study from 5:00 to 6:00 P.M. Domestic literacy instruction was an especially important part of the school's curriculum because it was the type of instruction that would teach the girls the "civilized habits" missionaries considered essential.

Religious literacy instruction was easily the most prominent and heavily emphasized part of the curriculum. According to Carr, during the opening exercises of school each morning, the girls who could would memorize the same verse from the Bible instead of having a scripture reading. Each girl started with the first chapter of the Book of John, which significantly begins, "In the beginning was the Word." Carr states that "Everyone was taught as far as possible to explain the meaning of the verse and give the definition of the most important words. They finished the Gospel some time before the school suspended." In the evenings, the students would repeat the verse they had memorized that morning. Also, any girl who wished could memorize a Bible verse of her own choosing and recite it at breakfast. Although this was not required, most of the girls and all of the teachers participated in this ritual.[26]

Reverend Carr preached at Bloomfield every other Sunday morning and led services in neighboring communities on the other Sundays. Sometimes, Reverend John Harrell, who was the superintendent of the Indian Missions, would preach in his place. Church services were primarily held in the schoolhouse, but occasionally they would be held outside "in an arbor near the branch, in the summertime." Carr writes that the students "were nature's children and much preferred to worship in God's universal temple. At these services the whole school was always in attendance." Bible classes were held for the older students in addition to regular church services. Mrs. Carr taught the advanced Bible class, and "her pupils would compare well with any children of the same opportunities in their understanding of the Scriptures." Younger students were first taught the catechism and, after they had successfully memorized it, advanced to Bible classes. Carr also states that singing was an integral part of the family worship.[27]

Religious study permeated the atmosphere at Bloomfield and was as much a part of the curriculum as academic or domestic study. The personal letters of two students and one teacher reveal just how significant religious studies were at Bloomfield. On April 3, 1857, Harriet Byrd of "Bloomfield Academy, C. N." (Chickasaw Nation) wrote these lines: "I presume you would like to know how much we are progressing in our studies; and in religion. The school is doing well and most of the girls have become interested in religion since you were here last. We are very much interested in our Sabbath lessons. We love to search the Scriptures, for in them we find the words of eternal life." Harriet Byrd's letter is very similar to Lorena Factor's, which she wrote on April 2 of the same year. Lorena spends time discussing the academic subjects but quickly moves to her religious goals: "I am still in school, and the subjects which I am pursuing are arithmetic, geography, United States History and botany; all of which interest me very much, especially history. I am trying to make the best possible use of these advantages, hoping that some day to be qualified to impart the instruction which I receive to those of my own people who are yet in ignorance and also to tell them of the love of Jesus." [28]

The following letter by Angelina Carr is interesting because it deals with the mission's primary purpose — conversion. The letter does not mention any other subject, perhaps because the baptism of several students was such an accomplishment for the missionaries that it overshadowed any other type of progress. On April 2, 1857, Angelina Hosmer Carr wrote: "Our dear brother McAlester preached here last Sabbath and assisted Mr. Carr at communion. It was a very solemn and interesting day for us all. Fifteen of our pupils united with the church; of these twelve were baptized, the other three having been baptized in infancy. Sister E. I. Downs, our new teacher, whom we were expecting when you were here, also joined the church by letter." [29]

Religion is the main topic of these letters; academic progress is secondary, if mentioned at all. Like the authors of the letters, Sarah Carr devotes the bulk of her narrative about Bloomfield, written in 1901, to spiritual matters. In her account of the school's activities, Carr spends ample time describing religious actives; however, she merely lists the academic subjects without describing how they were taught or going into depth about the progress made. Because the mission teachers' primary purpose was the "salvation of the people," her lengthy description of religious studies and activities is not surprising.[30] The missionaries used literacy education to aid in the "salvation" and "civilization" of the Chickasaws.

However, teaching the students white Christian traditions was not enough for the missionaries; stripping the students of Native traditions had to happen simultaneously. Lawrence Cremin points out that "Along with their formal classroom instruction, the missionaries were expected to work with the adults, on the one hand teaching them the reading and religion that would prepare them for conversion and on the other hand teaching them the ways of contemporary white agriculture and domestic economy." [31] Thomas Hartley Crawford, the commissioner of the Bureau of Indian Affairs from 1838 to 1845, addressed the important link between literacy and acculturation:

> They must at the least be taught to read and write, and have some acquaintance with figures; but if they do not learn to build and live in houses, to sleep on beds; to eat at regular intervals; to plow, and sow, and reap; to rear and use domestic animals; to understand and practise the mechanic arts; and to enjoy, to their gratification and improvement, all the means of profit and rational pleasure that are so profusely spread around civilized life, their mere knowledge of what is learned in the school room proper will be completely valueless. [32]

Carr's narrative verifies this philosophy. She does not spend much time describing the progress of the students in their academic, social, or even domestic classes; instead, large sections of her narrative are devoted to the progress made in religious literacy and in the habits of civilization. The missionaries made every effort to strip the students of their Native culture. In fact, one of the purposes of having boarding schools instead of neighborhood schools was so that the students would be removed from their families and other "heathenish" influences. The girls were not allowed to speak the Chickasaw language at school or, in the cases of many mixed-blood families, at home.

Sarah Carr describes the ways in which the missionaries helped change the customs of the Chickasaw people. She writes, "It is no easy task to persuade anyone that the way their ancestors did is not the very best way." For example, while the Carrs were at Bloomfield, polygamy was outlawed, and many couples were required to have a lawful marriage ceremony performed. She writes that "Many a couple, with children grown around them, stood up and made the solemn promise to cleave to each other 'so long as ye both shall live' as though they had not been doing so through all the years." Another example she cites was the method of burial in Indian Territory. It was the Chickasaw custom to bury their dead in their houses. The first Chickasaw was buried in the cemetery while the Carrs were there.[33]

Although Carr seems very proud of this progress, she writes about the Chickasaws with love, calling them "warm friends," not "heathens," and during the Carr administration in 1859, an older student at Bloomfield, Serena Factor, was invited to teach the primary grades until Rebecca Pritchett was hired in 1860. Carr writes that Serena was "honored and beloved by all. . . . The girls all called her 'cousin.' She was gentle and sweet in her disposition, a devout Christian and exercised a strong controling influence over the whole school." [34] The fact that Serena, a full-blood, was allowed to teach the primary grades indicates a good relationship between the missionaries and students at this time and says a great deal about the missionaries' attitude toward them.

The missionaries did accomplish their literacy goals; by the Civil War, most Chickasaws were converted to Christianity, and the missionaries helped establish education as a tradition among the Chickasaws, an important contribution. Historian Irene Mitchell writes: "They were able to transplant their love of wisdom in such manner as to endow their pupils not only with a keen awareness of righteous living, but also with the desire to learn. These teachers . . . created a cultured environment for the Indian children and influenced the social tone of the entire community." [35]

The Chickasaws, generally not in favor of the emphasis on religious literacy instruction at Bloomfield, had their own agenda. During the period of missionary control, the Chickasaws rebuilt their nation, solidifying and expanding their economic base and preparing their children to be leaders by providing literacy education for them. For the Chickasaws, literacy was a way to "equalize" and enable the Chickasaws to compete economically with the white settlers populating the region. The Chickasaws began their tradition of education in Mississippi and had done everything in their control to school their children, from sending them east to building schools themselves. They were proud of their accomplishments. Consequently, Bloomfield's commencement activities were celebrations.

Carr recalls that the school closed every year with a public examination, which was widely attended. Carr does not describe what sort of examinations were held or how long they lasted, but she does describe the size and nature of the commencement activities: "Many of the parents lived at a distance and those who had no relations in the neighborhood stayed all night with us the night before. All who attended the examination, whether living near or far away, were invited to dinner. Usually as many as three hundred dined with us on that day alone." [36] Commencement activities like the ones described were not uncommon in Indian Territory. The fact that so many people attended attests to the tremendous value the Chickasaws placed on the education of their children, female as well as male, an education they would soon control.

The War Years

Neither the missionaries nor the Chickasaws could have known that Bloomfield would soon close its doors. The outbreak of the Civil War in 1861 interrupted the plans of both parties and drastically altered life in Indian Territory. Both the Chickasaw and Choctaw Nations signed a treaty with the Confederacy; however, nearly 250 Chickasaws were sympathetic to the Union and fled to Kansas, where they stayed throughout the war. [37] The fathers of many Bloomfield students immediately enlisted with the Confederacy and took their daughters home for the duration of the war. The Chickasaw Battalion was ordered to move into Bloomfield and used the schoolhouse as a hospital and the sitting room as a commissary. Most of the soldiers camped on the prairie surrounding the school. [38] Historians Leland Clegg and William Oden discuss the hardships of the war years, hardships many don't associate with Indian Territory: "It would be painful even to write of the atrocities committed toward the Indians during the war. All the horrors of the Civil War were found in Indian Territory — looting, fire, murder, rape. There were inter-tribal conflicts and rival councils set up."[39]

In spite of the terrible conditions, many missionaries, including John and Sarah Carr, stayed on in Indian Territory. Near Bloomfield, John Carr opened a free neighborhood school, which was open three hours every morning. Sarah Carr writes that no missionaries received any sort of salary during the war; they subsisted on whatever they could produce themselves. According to her, "There was no hope of Missionary operation being resumed for years to come."[40] At the end of the Civil War, the Indian Mission Conference was indeed in shambles. The board was badly in debt and had little money to pay for the salaries of its missionaries or for the reconstruction of schools, many of which had been destroyed or severely damaged. Furthermore, many missionaries had been working in Indian Territory since the days of removal and chose to end their careers. The Indian Mission Conference did continue some activities, but in a very limited way.[41] In 1867, John Carr took his new wife, Sarah Johnson Carr, and their children and moved to Paris, Texas, to make a living, thus ending Bloomfield's missionary years.

The Golden Age

After the Civil War, the Chickasaws were once again faced with the rebuilding of their nation, their businesses, and their schools. Reorganizing the schools was not an easy task, and this time the Chickasaws would do it alone. The missionaries were gone, and the Chickasaws took full advantage of the opportunity for complete control. For once in Bloomfield's history, the Chickasaw's literacy agenda was the only agenda. This is especially remarkable when placed in national context. The Chickasaws took control of their schools in 1865 and would keep control until 1907. Carlisle Indian Industrial School, the first off-reservation boarding school in the country for Indians, did not open until 1879. Too many children of other tribes were taken too far from their homes and placed in federally run off-reservation boarding schools, schools that were certainly not interested in the opinions of the tribes. The Chickasaws had their own schools and controlled their own schools — schools located in the Chickasaw Nation in Chickasaw communities. It is no wonder that the period of Chickasaw control has been called the golden age of Bloomfield by Oklahoma historians and Bloomfield alumnae and their descendants.[42]

The years between the end of the war in 1865 and 1876 are sketchy. The Treaty of 1866 with the United States reestablished the governments of both the Chickasaw and Choctaw Nations and outlined the terms of their Reconstruction programs.[43] The Chickasaws' primary concern was the reorganization of their schools, and they appropriated the majority of their funds to subsidize their twelve neighborhood day schools. The school buildings were in such a state of disrepair that they could not be used, and the Chickasaws did not have enough money to rebuild immediately; consequently, the old academies were not reopened as boarding schools until after 1876.[44]

Although the Chickasaws adopted a new constitution in 1867, specifically stating that their children should be provided with a quality education, their schools were not well organized and were "largely conducted upon the personal responsibility and individual of the person in charge."[45] The administration of the Bloomfield school changed hands several times between 1865 and 1876. At the close of the war, Captain Frederic Young of the Confederate Army opened a neighborhood school in the Bloomfield building that both boys and girls attended while the Chickasaws reorganized. An accidental fire destroyed the buildings; however, the neighborhood school continued operating elsewhere. In 1867 the Chickasaws rebuilt the school, this time of frame and brick instead of logs.[46]

In 1868, Dr. and Mrs. H. F. Murray took over the superintendentship of the school. Mrs. Murray, who had been educated in Salem, North Carolina, was originally from Mississippi and was a member of a prominent Chickasaw family. Dr. Murray was a physician and retained his practice during his administration of Bloomfield. The couple was considered well educated and culturally refined. Mrs. Murray bought the school its first piano; music was considered a vital part of the school's curriculum thereafter. The Murrays were succeeded by Professor Robert Cole in 1870. Cole acted as superintendent for the following five years and established high school grades.[47]

Between 1865 and 1876, the individual superintendents of Bloomfield essentially did whatever they saw fit. The truly golden years of Bloomfield began in 1876, when the Chickasaws, having fully reorganized their government, turned to the organization of their school system and made their purposes for Bloomfield clear. A school report, published in 1873, shows the nation's desire to raise the standards of their schools and their reasons for doing so. The report states that the schools should "be carried on in a manner that would reflect honor on the Nation, besides conferring a lasting good upon the rising generation . . . and in their belief we ask the help and support of every sober thinking mind of our country. Let us inaugurate schools that will elevate our children to an equal footing with our white brethren." [48]

In 1876, the Chickasaws acted on those desires, and their governor, Benjamin Franklin Overton, signed a law establishing a female seminary at Bloomfield Academy. Professor J. E. Wharton was named superintendent of Bloomfield, which would be completely run under the auspices of the Chickasaw Nation; all missionary contact was excluded. Furthermore, the law stipulated that the school would be contracted out to a superintendent of "the highest moral character, or Christian standing, with practical and successful experience in teaching and managing a first-class boarding school." Significantly, the law established entrance requirements for the seminary, which stated that "no student shall enter said seminary until they can read well in McGuffey's Fifth Reader, spell well, and read in the New Testament, and be of good moral character." [49] The enrollment of the seminary was capped at forty-five students; no family was allowed to send more than one child, and the child could attend for a total of five years.[50]

Governor Overton signed two other significant laws regarding education in 1876. One act authorized the superintendent of public instruction to issue certificates and designated a standard set of textbooks for each school. The second act authorized the punishment of persons who attempted to decoy children away from school.[51] All three of the laws show the Chickasaw Nation's interest in the betterment of their schools. Governor Benjamin Crooks Burney shared Governor Overton's interest and in 1879 stated that "Education is the lever by which our people are to be raised to a mental level with our surroundings, and I desire to seriously impress upon you how important it is that you use your influence in getting our people to see to the education of the young."[52]

Robert Boyd, a member of the Chickasaw Nation, succeeded Professor J. E. Wharton as superintendent in 1880. Boyd left in 1882, and the superintendentship was taken over by Douglas H. Johnston, a former student of the Bloomfield neighborhood school after the Civil War and the son-in-law of Serena Factor, one of Bloomfield's first students and teachers.[53] In 1888, the Bloomfield Academy buildings were condemned, and the Chickasaw Council passed an act to build a new academy in Panola County, Texas. Unfortunately the new school was destroyed by fire in 1896. The Panola school was rebuilt, in the same place as the previous one.[54] Elihu B. Hinshaw served as principal under Johnston and succeeded him as superintendent in 1896. Hinshaw was considered an outstanding educator and held A.B. and M.A. degrees. He was a pharmacist, lecturer, lawyer, and author and eventually became the vice-president of the Southeastern Normal School at Durant, Oklahoma.[55]

A historical account of Bloomfield Academy published by the Chickasaw Nation holds that Bloomfield "reached its highest peak as an educational institution and a seat of culture during the Johnston and Hinshaw administrations."[56] The Chickasaws took full advantage of their period of control. Their purpose was to "inaugurate schools that will elevate our children to an equal footing with our white brethren." For the Chickasaws, the purpose of literacy was not to "Christianize" but to "equalize." The Chickasaw had a different literacy agenda than the missionaries and changed the literacy curriculum of Bloomfield accordingly. Although religious literacy was certainly not the focus of instruction under Chickasaw control, it was not entirely absent. The students did attend church services every Sunday as well as Sunday school classes, which were taught by the school's teachers. Furthermore, the ritual of beginning each day's work with the reading of a scripture continued.[57] The laws enacted by the Chickasaw Council required teachers, administrators, and students to be of good moral character or Christian, demonstrating that although missionaries were not a strong force in Indian Territory after the Civil War, their legacy continued; most Chickasaws were Christian, and Christian values were an integral part of the school.

The academic literacy curriculum was much more stringent than under missionary control. The Chickasaws set entrance requirements for Bloomfield, and because basic literacy was one of those requirements, Bloomfield could offer more subjects and at a more advanced level. More students were able to meet the entrance requirements because of the early work of the missionaries and because many of the students were mixed-blood and had at least one parent that spoke English. Language barriers were, in all likelihood, not as significant a problem as they had been in the missionary years. However, Johnston made a significant effort to increase the enrollment of full-blood students, and during his administration the Chickasaw Legislature made a grant of ten dollars per month "for the maintenance of each pupil, whether living at home or boarding at Bloomfield."[58] As a result, more and more families moved within the surrounding area of Bloomfield, and the poorer families were able to educate their daughters at Bloomfield.

If the academic literacy curriculum was rigorous, it was due largely to the efforts of Professor Hinshaw, who developed an improved course of study for Bloomfield students and submitted it to the Chickasaw Legislature for approval. The legislators were so pleased with the new plan that they showed their approval by issuing a charter to Bloomfield that authorized it to award diplomas to graduating students. Bloomfield was the only one of the Chickasaw academies to receive this privilege. Furthermore, graduates of Bloomfield were immediately considered eligible to teach at any of the schools in the Chickasaw Nation without passing any teacher examinations.[59] Some Bloomfield graduates did become Bloomfield teachers, demonstrating that an academy education could significantly widen the scope of possibilities for Indian women, just as it had for white northeastern women.

The academic literacy curriculum offered at Bloomfield under Chickasaw control was considered "equal to the course of study offered in present day junior colleges" and included advanced subjects such as logic, chemistry, astronomy, and botany as well as more traditional courses such as spelling, reading, writing, arithmetic, geography, English grammar, U.S. history, physiology, rhetoric, civil government, natural philosophy, general history, algebra, and American literature.[60] Classes in English composition and literature, mythology, and Latin and Caesar were also offered. Some of the books used include "Steele's Science and Astronomy, Barnes' Historical Series, Reed and Kellogg's Grammar, then Rhetoric, Ray's Arithmetic, and Wentworth's Geometry."[61] The Chickasaw Nation furnished all of the textbooks. The academy also had "a good library, including encyclopedias, latest standard works in history and science, and choice literature."[62]

The school's good reputation was not only due to the high academic standards. During the Johnston and Hinshaw administrations the school was sometimes referred to as the "Bryn Mawr of the West." It was considered a privilege to attend Bloomfield, and graduates, who "enjoyed a measure of prestige," were known as the Bloomfield Blossoms.[63]

The Chickasaws' economic security depended on negotiation and trade with white communities; their national security depended on their relationship with the U.S. government. Consequently, many Chickasaws found themselves having to compete in a white world and needed their daughters to be "cultured" and "refined," able to negotiate social and economic boundaries. Many students were trying to achieve social literacy so that they could participate in both the white community and in the Chickasaw community as role models and leaders. Perhaps the type of literacy education offered Bloomfield students under Chickasaw control is best termed "effective literacy."[64] The students were trained to become Republican Mothers and "True Women" who could effect change in their own lives and in the lives of others and help to ensure the survival of the Chickasaw Nation through that change.

Professor Hinshaw placed tremendous emphasis on the fine arts, and the social literacy curriculum was the most prominent part of the curriculum at this time in the school's history. Bloomfield's social literacy instruction included physical culture, oil painting, pastel, charcoal, and pen work, piano, guitar, mandolin, violin, banjo, voice, and elocution. During the period of Chickasaw control Bloomfield also had active extracurricular organizations that included an orchestra and glee club as well as a library society, basketball teams, and a group know as the Indian Club Swingers.[65] The art department was considered especially strong, and the work of Bloomfield students was exhibited at the Louisiana Purchase Exposition held in St. Louis in 1904 and was awarded a prize.[66]

Hinshaw placed such emphasis on the social literacy curriculum that the following letterhead was used on Bloomfield stationery: "Bloomfield Seminary. Literary, Music, Art, Elocution. A School for the Higher Education of Chickasaw Indian Girls and Young Ladies."[67] That final phrase exemplifies Hinshaw's purpose. Notes from his lectures also show the stress he placed on social literacy. The following quotes were taken from the class notes of Nettie Burris:

Be dignified and cultured young ladies.
Be a graduate of some institution.
Do not tease whatever you do.
Away with selfishness, we are not living for selves alone but for the happiness of those with whom we come in contact.
You will want to be measured by your success.
Higher up the cherry tree grows the cherry.
Have it said that you are from Bloomfield.[68]

The class notes demonstrate that the Bloomfield Blossoms were striving toward True Womanhood, an ideal of the late nineteenth century that placed women on pedestals as pious and pure, domestic and dutiful.[69] The ideals of True Womanhood are manifested in every aspect of the social literacy curriculum, and lines from the poem "The World of Women," which was included in a commencement program from the

Hinshaw administration, could almost be viewed as a mission statement or class motto:

> Be a woman — on to duty,
> Raise the world from all that's low,
>
> .   .   .
>
> Be not fashion's gilded lady,
> Be a brave, whole-souled, true woman![70]

Commencement, always an important tradition at Bloomfield, was not just a celebration during this period — it was one of the most important social events in the Chickasaw Nation. Rigorous oral and written examinations came first. The examinations were public, and parents and friends were allowed to participate in the questioning of the students.[71] Examinations were reputed to last several days. Bloomfield, which historians have called "a seat of culture" and "the cultural institution in the southern part of Indian Territory," held graduation exercises and huge celebrations afterward that included entertainment, usually in the form of a play or musical presentation, and feasting.[72] Newspaper reporters covering the event made a point of listing the most prominent guests and detailing the events of the day.

Because the commencement exercises were considered major social occasions, each year students made their own graduation dresses, which were considered to be the height of fashion. The class of 1904 chose white Japanese silk for their identical, ankle-length gowns; they were considered "fashion plates of loveliness." The students also wore black mortar-board academic caps, which were embroidered with the initials "B.B." (Bloomfield Blossoms) in bright yellow.[73] It has also been said that the caps were embroidered with a blossom.

All students participated in the music and literary program that was presented to the audience. Each member of the graduating class was required to write and present an original essay at commencement.[74] The following reproduction of the 1904 commencement program reveals a great deal about the social literacy curriculum emphasized at Bloomfield under Chickasaw control.

INVOCATION.

Chorus—"Summer Fancies"............................. Metra
Glee Club.

Salutatory—"The Development of the Indian Territory."
Lucy Young.

Class Recitation—"Wind."

Orchestra—"Zacatecas" .... Cordina

Essay—"Helen Keller"........................... Jane Newberry

Piano (30 hands)—"Les Amazones".................... Streabog
Carrie Love, Neta Johnston, Carrie Young, Melissa
Johnson, Sudie Durham, Lucy White, Grace
Moore, Lizie Grinslade, Effie Archerd,
Illa White, Jennie Connelly, Rowena
Burks, Eddie Turnbull, Elsie
Reynolds, Lorena Eastman.

Poem—"The Lotus Eaters" .... Tennyson
Pantomimed by Class; Reading, Carrie Young.

Orchestra—"March Edina"........................... Wiegand
Essay—"Our Alma Mater."
Charlotte Goforth.

Chorus—"A Natural Spell" .... Bristow
Glee Club.

Piano (16 hands)—"La Premier Danseuse" .... Zetterbait
Myrtle Conner, Sophia Frye, Vera Burks, Cecil
Burris, Lena Thompson, Minnie Good,
Fannie Kemp, Ramona Bynum.

Essay—"A Rough Surface, Polished, Shines Forth in Brilliancy."
Myrtle Conner.

Chorus—"Morn Rise"................................. Czebulka
Glee Club.

Solo (5 pianos)—"Invitation to a Dance" .... Weber
(op. 65.)
Charlotte Goforth, Lucy Young, Bertie Smith,
Lucretia Harris, Rennie Colbert.

Essay—"History Making of the Present Age."
Ramona Bynum.

Duet (4 pianos)—"June Bugs"............................ Holst
Lillie Sacra, Daisy Harris, Illa White, Ruth Easkey,
Zula Wolfenbarger, Josie McGeehee,
Lena Thompson, Abbie Mead.

Orchestra—"Valse Ninette" .... Bosce

Piano (quartette)—"Grand March" .... Wallenhaupt
Charlotte Goforth, Lucy Young, Bertie
Smith, Lucretia Harris.

Valedictory—"Peace On Earth."
Bertie Smith.

Graduating Ode—"Dear Sisters, Now Adieu".............. Ayres
Seniors and Juniors.

Presentation of Certificates and Diplomas.

Orchestra.[75]

As evidenced by the program, the students were required to study canonical literature and poetry and the performing and fine arts, a strong social literacy curriculum that led to Bloomfield's reputation as a cultural hub. Historian Irene Mitchell writes, "Music and drama at Bloomfield Academy were a part of the culture and had a lasting influence upon life in the Chickasaw Nation. . . . This cultural heritage among the Chickasaws received from the graduates of Bloomfield left its impress in the state of Oklahoma."[76]

Conspicuously absent from every list of courses and activities are cooking, housekeeping, and sewing, staples of a domestic literacy curriculum. The fact that the students made their own graduation dresses is the only evidence that homemaking skills may have been part of the curriculum during this period. The emphasis on social literacy and the lack of emphasis on domestic literacy is due to the Chickasaw's mission for Bloomfield. The students at Bloomfield under Chickasaw control no longer needed the lessons in "civilization" that the missionaries provided; now they wanted lessons in refinement. Chickasaws did not provide literacy education for their daughters so they could become the servants of white women. Bloomfield Blossoms received literacy instruction so they could become the wives of leaders in the nation and leaders in the community. Bloomfield students needed social literacy instruction so that they would be prepared to participate in both Indian and white communities and help Chickasaws transcend significant social and economic boundaries.

The literacy education they received is particularly interesting because it was based on a model of True Womanhood and Republican Motherhood, the latter based on the ideal of being a mother in the republic of the United States who will raise her children to be good citizens of that republic. Bloomfield students were members of and lived in the Chickasaw Nation in Indian Territory and even addressed their letters accordingly. They were under the protection of the United States to some extent but were not citizens of that republic. Of what nation were Chickasaw girls being trained to become citizens? They lived in an Indian nation, in the middle of a white nation. Many of the students were mixed-blood and had both white and Chickasaw family members. Many spoke both the Chickasaw and the English languages. Chickasaw students were truly mixing languages and mixing cultures and orchestrated their own identities to accommodate this mix. They received a literacy education that would enable them to participate as citizens of the Chickasaw Nation in Indian Territory in the United States. An ability to draw on different literacies helped students to participate in the Chickasaw community and in the white community, and at that particular place at that particular time, their world was a mixture of both.

The records and articles I have found regarding the curriculum and life at Bloomfield indicate that preserving the Chickasaw language and heritage was most likely not on the educational agenda. It would be a mistake, however, to suggest that elements of Chickasaw culture were never present. For example, a 1904 quarterly report lists students who participated in the "Indian Club Swingers."[77] A newspaper article, which lists the foods served at the commencement feast, mentions *tah ful la*, a popular Chickasaw dish.[78] The 1904 commencement program lists the reading of an essay on the development of Indian Territory.[79] But those instances are minor. Traditional Chickasaw culture was certainly not taught and perhaps discouraged at Bloomfield; however, at this early date, Chickasaw culture was not lost in the community. Students who attended school during the era of Chickasaw control did not face the same loss of traditional cultural heritage as students who attended after Oklahoma statehood, in the next generations, because the old ways, though evolving, were still all around them.

However, living cultures do change, and customs and traditions do evolve into new traditions. The huge commencement celebrations Bloomfield and the other academies held were in all likelihood transposed versions of other much older traditional ceremonies and feasts. For many Chickasaws, education had become a tradition, and celebrating it may have enabled them, significantly, to continue the traditional rituals of coming together as a community, sharing stories, and feasting. "New" traditions may not have been all that new; they may have been very important links to old ways and, consequently, to continuance. By changing, the Chickasaws were not becoming "less Indian" but were proving that their culture was dynamic and thriving. For that matter, how could Chickasaw people be any *more* Chickasaw? Chickasaws lived on their own land in the Chickasaw Nation. They were self-governing and, to a great extent, self-sufficient. In the sixty years since their removal, they had rebuilt their nation and achieved a tremendous and truly unique level of autonomy. The Chickasaws, in control, defined what it meant to be Chickasaw.

Twilight

Unfortunately, the Chickasaws were not allowed to keep control of their educational system for long. The U.S. government took control of the schools and appointed a superintendent for Indian Territory with the passage of the Curtis Act in 1898.[80] The final years of Bloomfield under Chickasaw control were years of struggle; Oklahoma statehood was imminent, and federal government officials were already trying to take over the schools, much to the dismay of Chickasaws who were proud of what they had accomplished at Bloomfield and their other academies and neighborhood schools.

Chickasaw leaders fought the takeover for several years and used every maneuver they could to keep control; however, they could do nothing because the secretary of interior took control of their funds. Historian Joe Jackson states that the Indian nations were forced to "cooperate with the inevitable," and that "Under Federal control many outward forms were left unchanged. In fact, it was not unusual to leave popular Indian leaders in important administrative positions. However, there was never any doubt as to where the ultimate source of authority was lodged."[81]

At the turn of the century, the Chickasaw Nation operated thirteen day schools, four academies, and an orphans' home. By contrast, rural whites living in the boundaries of the Chickasaw Nation "had to depend on scattered, poorly taught and poorly equipped subscription schools." By statehood in 1907, the government had laid the necessary groundwork for a state educational system by using the school systems of the Five Civilized Tribes as "blue prints," and 996 day schools, which white students could attend, were already in operation.[82] Government officials quickly found reasons to shut down the Chickasaws' school system and with it the old academies. Bloomfield Academy, the pride of the Chickasaws, would remain in operation, but out of their control.

4

Eho inanaumpolit (The Women's Story)
Bloomfield Academy and Carter Seminary
under Federal Control

❉

I will tell you something about stories. . . . They aren't just for entertainment. Don't be fooled. They are all we have, you see. . . . You don't have anything if you don't have the stories. — LESLIE MARMON SILKO, *Ceremony*

The summer of 1996 was unlike any other summer of my life. I seemed to spend every weekend driving around Oklahoma, many times with my father and sometimes my mother, too, to the homes of women who attended Bloomfield or Carter. I was getting to know my relatives. Those were good days — summertime mornings or afternoons spinning out, one hour turning into two, then three — long conversations over lunch or dinner or ice cold tea. Daddy and his cousins would talk and laugh, telling the old stories and poking through shoeboxes and albums full of old pictures. I listened. I had never heard many of these stories. People forget to tell them sometimes. But stories are important, and I heard lots of stories that summer, not just from relatives, but from other women as well. I made quite a few new friends. I learned that listening to stories is as important as telling them and that shared stories and sharing stories are what make a family a family and a community a community. The students at Bloomfield and Carter became both to each other, family and community. I am not sure that is what policymakers intended to happen, but it did.

The school changed drastically after statehood in 1907. Government officials had different objectives for literacy education than the Chickasaws or the missionaries and changed the curriculum of the school accordingly. Many of the women I had the opportunity to talk with were aware of those objectives even as children. Others came to their conclusions about their school experiences later, as adults. All remember their school days well; they have given these days some thought over the years.

I listened to their stories and would like to include some of them here. We have already heard the voices of reformers, missionaries and teachers, and legislators. The voices of the students, the people who were the most deeply affected, have often been the softest — not because they do not have a lot to say. They talked about the Chickasaw Nation and about being a Chickasaw woman in Oklahoma. I understood that they, too, had a stake in their own education and had their own ideas about what sorts of lives they should and would lead. By listening to them, I got some idea of what it was like to be a girl, a mixed-blood girl, growing up in Oklahoma in the first part of this century and some sense of just how different things were for Chickasaw people after statehood and why. This is what they told me.

The Struggle for Control

The Chickasaws fought to maintain control of Bloomfield as long as they could, but they were really fighting a much larger battle — a battle they had no hope of winning. White settlers demanded more land, believed it was their destiny to have the land, and would not be denied. Christian reformers and legislators knew certainly that the current reservation system could not last; they, too, believed that the western frontier, all of it, would and should be settled. Furthermore, the cycle of dependency and poverty that the reservation system had created was disastrous. Reformers and legislators wanted to develop policies that would solve the "Indian problem" immediately and, hopefully, permanently. Coming up with an answer was easy enough — civilizing the

Indians seemed to be the perfect solution. Coming up with workable implementation strategies proved much more difficult. After much debate, reformers and legislators developed a three-pronged plan. They agreed to extend the nation's legal system to Indians, break up reservations for the allotment of land in severalty, and provide Indians with a complete and systematized educational system.

Providing Indians with individual land allotments was hardly a new idea, but it was one in which most policymakers had great confidence. As Francis Paul Prucha points out, "It was an article of faith with the reformers that civilization was impossible without the incentive to work that came only from individual ownership of a piece of property." [1] Not every legislator agreed; nonetheless, Congress passed the General Allotment Act, also known as the Dawes Act, in 1887. [2] The act simultaneously made Indians individual property owners and citizens, thus, striking a blow for "civilization," and liquidated reservations for white settlement. The Chickasaws, Choctaws, Cherokees, Creeks, and Seminoles in Indian Territory were in a unique situation. They had been removed to Indian Territory with the promise that they would be protected from white settlers and state governments and allowed to self-govern and live as they chose. [3] The Dawes Act was in direct violation of their treaty agreements, a fact delegates of these tribal nations quickly made known. As a result of their efforts, the Dawes Act of 1887 did not apply to the southeastern nations in Indian Territory.

Their reprieve would not last long. The Five Civilized Tribes had their own lands, governments, legal systems, businesses, and schools. The semi-autonomous nations in Indian Territory made Congress uncomfortable, as did the fact that every one of them had allied with the Confederacy during the Civil War. The idea that the Indian nations might exist forever in Indian Territory seemed impossible and even absurd to government officials. [4] Significantly, there was some discussion among tribal leaders and legislators about the possibility of the Five Civilized Tribes joining together to form one territorial government that, like other organized U.S. territories, would receive representation in Congress and eventually become a state. [5] Although legislators were generally amenable to that plan, tribal members were not. Citizens of the Indian nations were at least as patriotic as citizens of the United States and consequently refused to surrender their own national identities by banding together. Congress then established the Dawes Commission, chaired by Senator Henry Dawes, to negotiate with the Five Civilized Tribes. Tribal delegates basically refused to negotiate, and in their 1894 report, the Dawes Commission severely criticized the conditions in Indian Territory, thereby providing a rationale for the United States to disregard promises made in the removal treaties.[6]

For the Chickasaws, the Dawes Act did not mean just the liquidation of their land; it meant the literal termination of their government, of their status as a semi-autonomous nation. Chickasaw leaders refuted the claims made in the report of the Dawes Commission and fought allotment in every way they could, but they were outmatched. In 1897, Chickasaw and Choctaw leaders signed the Atoka Agreement, which stipulated that their tribal governments would terminate on March 4, 1906, and that tribal citizens would become citizens of the United States. Chickasaw voters rejected the Atoka Agreement, but their rejection was overridden when Congress adopted the Curtis Act in 1898, which effectively ended all negotiations.[7] According to historian Arrell Gibson, the Curtis Act, which definitively answered the "Indian question" and paved the way for Oklahoma statehood, "consolidated those laws which erased tribal autonomy and authorized the survey and platting of Indian Territory town sites and the sale of town lots. It made provision for the incorporation of towns and the creation of municipal governments including elections. Tribal trust funds were to be liquidated through per capita payments and all tribal governments were to terminate on March 4, 1906."[8]

The Dawes Commission began the long process of implementing the allotment policy by creating tribal rolls; only enrolled tribal members could receive allotments. Tribal enrollment had several significant implications. The Dawes Commission was in charge of enrollment; therefore, the Chickasaws lost one of their most basic rights — the right to decide their own membership. Furthermore, the enrollment process

My grandmother, Ida Mae Pratt Cobb (Dinah) in her school uniform, c. 1925.

Students and faculty of the first of four Bloomfield Academy buildings, c. 1852–60. Note the variety of ages among the students. The school was destroyed by fire several times in its history. Photo #226.4, courtesy of the Oklahoma Historical Society.

One of the few photographs of the second Bloomfield Academy building with students and faculty, taken c. 1890–92. Note the more formal architectural design. Photo #1316, T. W. Hunter Collection, courtesy of the Oklahoma Historical Society.

This photograph of Bloomfield Academy students and faculty appears to have been taken at the second academy building. It seems to represent the higher number of apparently mixed-blood students as compared to the later years. Photo #4, W. Hill Collection, courtesy of the Western History Collections, University of Oklahoma Library.

The third Bloomfield Academy building, near Achille, Oklahoma, in 1908, one year after Oklahoma statehood. Built during the golden age of Bloomfield, the period of Chickasaw control, this building amply reflects Bloomfield's reputation as the "cultural seat" of Indian Territory in the late 1800s. Photo #75.39.54, courtesy of the Oklahoma Historical Society.

Students and faculty at the third Bloomfield Academy building, c. 1896–1900, during the height of the school's popularity. The large number of students in this picture demonstrates the capacity enrollments Bloomfield maintained during this period. Photo by Moore, Denison, Texas, photo #18439.1, courtesy of the Oklahoma Historical Society.

Miss Estelle Chisolm's class at Bloomfield in 1892. Seated in the foreground are E. B. Hinshaw, left, the school's principal at this time, and Douglas Johnston, right, the school's superintendent. Hinshaw succeeded Johnston as superintendent in 1896. Johnston was elected governor of the Chickasaw Nation in 1898. The school was said to have reached its "high-water mark" of excellence under their administrations. Johnston was the son-in-law of Serena Factor, one of the school's first students and its first Chickasaw teacher. Photo #3, Litton Collection, courtesy of the Western History Collections, University of Oklahoma Library.

The Bloomfield Blossoms playing basketball on the Bloomfield grounds in the 1890s. It is said that Bloomfield had the first organized basketball team in the state of Oklahoma. The team was organized by one of the school's teachers, Mr. Light, who once coached basketball at the University of Notre Dame. Superintendent Hinshaw, a strict Quaker, objected to the girls being photographed in their bloomers; consequently, the girls are very well dressed for their basketball game. Photo #10585.B, Juanita Johnston Smith Collection, courtesy of the Oklahoma Historical Society.

During the 1890s, the school was regarded as a finishing school for young ladies, a mission accurately reflected in this photograph of the Bloomfield Blossoms in white dresses showing off their elaborately dressed hair. Note the flowers at each girl's feet. Photo # P-60.3L, courtesy of the Oklahoma Historical Society.

A Bloomfield music class, c. 1890s. Classes in music, art, elocution, and literature were the most prominent part of Bloomfield's curriculum in the 1890s. Bloomfield Blossoms were encouraged to be refined and cultured young ladies in every way. Photo #97.03.4, donated by L. T. Moody, courtesy of the Chickasaw Council House Museum, Tishomingo, Oklahoma.

After fire destroyed the third Bloomfield Academy building in 1914, the school was relocated to its fourth and final site—the Old Hargrove College in Ardmore, Oklahoma. Because the college needed many repairs, Bloomfield did not reopen until 1917. This photograph of the main building of Hargrove College was taken prior to statehood in 1907. N. W. Ardmore, I. T., photo #1289, courtesy of the William A. McGalliard Collection, Ardmore Public Library, Ardmore, Oklahoma.

Girls at Carter Seminary in the 1940s, still in white dresses, watch their classmates play a game of basketball. Unlike their 1890s counterparts, these basketball players were allowed to wear pants for the picture. Note how extensively the main building has been renovated since the turn of the century. Courtesy of Clara Pittman Gatlin, Mary Pittman Parris, Ula Mae Pittman Welch, and Josie Pittman Gage.

Teacher Van Noy Hughes, remembered by students as a favorite, appears in the center of the back row in this photograph of Carter Seminary students taken c. 1940–45. "Aunt Noy," a Bloomfield alum, was the sister of Fanny Hughes Bass and Ida Bell Hughes Martin, women whom I interviewed for this book. Four other women I interviewed are pictured. Claudine Williford King is front row center. Ula Mae Pittman Welch is seated directly below Van Noy. Fannye Williford Skaggs is in the back row, third from the end on the right. Dorothy Wall Holt is fourth from the end, next to Fannye. Courtesy of Clara Pittman Gatlin, Mary Pittman Parris, Ula Mae Pittman Welch, and Josie Pittman Gage.

This picture of Dorothy Wall Holt, taken by the Pittman sisters c. 1940s, captures the feelings of nostalgia many students expressed for their school days and their school friends. Nearly every woman I interviewed referred to her classmates as her "family" or "sisters." The stories of Dorothy Wall Holt, Clara Pittman Gatlin, Mary Pittman Parris, and Ula Mae Pittman Welch are included in this book. Courtesy of Clara Pittman Gatlin, Mary Pittman Parris, Ula Mae Pittman Welch, and Josie Pittman Gage.

WISTARIA

Carter Seminary students, c. 1940s, participate in a community parade. Students in the Carter Seminary orchestra or glee club frequently performed for Ardmore community organizations. Courtesy of Dorothy Wall Holt, Bloomfield Alumni Association.

Students in a Thanksgiving Day pageant at Carter Seminary in the 1940s. Like students elsewhere, Bloomfield and Carter students remember participating in school plays and assemblies, functions frequently designed to engender patriotism and citizenship. Pauline Williford Adkins, whom I interviewed for this book, is the second student on the left. Courtesy of Dorothy Wall Holt, Bloomfield Alumni Association.

A page from the Bloomfield/Carter Alumni Association guest register. My grandmother, Ida Mae Pratt Cobb, attended this reunion and signed her name on May 20, 1978.

DATE	NAME	ADDRESS	Bloomfield / Carter	Years Attended
5-20-78	Killa Sam	P.O. Box 803 McAlester, Okla.	—	guest
5-20-78	Louisa Sam	P.O. Box 803 McAlester, Okla.	—	guest
5-20-78	Oliver Carroll	1408 West Broadway, Hargrove	College	1941-42
5-20-78	Jay Erwin	1307 11th N.E.	Carter employee	1949-1961
5-20-78	Mr & Mrs. P.W. Frick	732 St Joseph Dr. Ada		Guest
5-20-78	Mr. & Mrs. Fred Johnson	1418 Ed 4 st, Ed Ada		Band
5-20-78	Michael Price	1207 S. Oak, Waurika Okla	Carter	1938-40
5-20-78	Minerva Hawkins	P O Box 226 Tecumseh Okla	Carter	1933-39
5-20-78	Ida Pratt Cobb	Box 99 Lehannahka	Bloomfield	1924-25
5-20-78	Frances B. Robinson	106 E. Burney	Bloomfield	1925-28
5-20-78	Sophia (Rula) Perry	Rt. 1 Stonewall 74871	Bloomfield	1923-28
5-20-78	Hazel (Bryan) Band	R1 Box 174 Wakita 73790	Bloomfield	1924-25
5-20-78	Arthur Griffin Broadie	P.O. 2 Box 119 Atoka Okla 74525	Bloomfield	1925, 1933
5-20-78	Dorothy (Well) Brief	704 E Bird, Davis Enid Okla	Carter	1998-47
5-20-78	Mary Lou Wall	Box 865 Davis Okla	Murray	1932-42
5-2	Ruby Bucher	825 Campbell NW Ardmore Okla 73401		
5-	Lillie Beasley	Ada	Guest Band	
5-	Dennie Marrian	Ada	Guest	
5-	Delia Milly	Ada	Guest	
41	Viola C Perry	Ada	Guest	
42	Peggy Everts	Ada	Guest	
43	Oneda Walker	Ada, Guest Band		
44	Marguerite Grind	Ada	Guest	
45	Corrine White	Ada C R Hoyt		
46	Bertha Price	Ada - Guest		

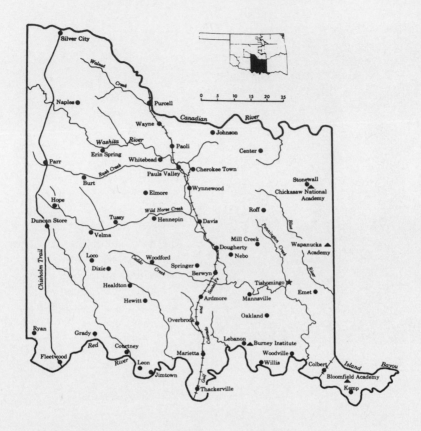

Chickasaw Nation: Important Places. Map no. 43 in John W. Morris, Charles R. Goins, and Edwin C. McReynolds, *Historical Atlas of Oklahoma*, 3rd ed. (Norman: University of Oklahoma Press). © 1976 by the University of Oklahoma Press.

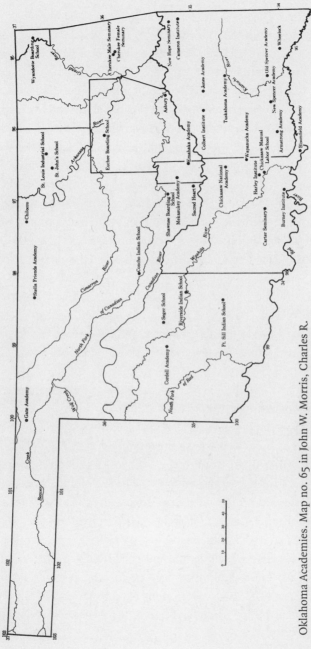

Oklahoma Academies. Map no. 65 in John W. Morris, Charles R. Goins, and Edwin C. McReynolds, *Historical Atlas of Oklahoma*, 3rd ed. (Norman: University of Oklahoma Press). © 1976 by the University of Oklahoma Press.

Wyandotte Boarding School

Cherokee Male Seminary
Cherokee Female Seminary

New Hope Seminary
Cameron Institute

Old Spencer Academy
Wheelock

Jones Academy

Tushkahoma Academy

New Spencer Academy

St. Louis Industrial School
St. John's School

Euchee Boarding School

Asbury

Emahaka Academy

Colbert Institute

Wapanucka Academy

Chickasaw Manual Labor School

Armstrong Academy
Bloomfield Academy

Chilocco

Sacred Heart

Shawnee Boarding School
Mekusukey Academy

Chickasaw National Academy

Harley Institute

Stella Friends Academy

Concho Indian School

Carter Seminary

Burney Institute

Seger School
Riverside Indian School

Ft. Sill Indian School

Gate Academy

Cordell Academy

was based on racial classification and identified tribal members by their quantum of Indian blood. Consequently, the Dawes Commission not only decided who was Chickasaw but just how Chickasaw a person was, thus setting up a system by which outsiders could judge someone's personal and ethnic identity. Government officials used the system of racial classification to maintain some control over Indian land by creating two classes of citizens, restricted and unrestricted. Restricted citizens, who usually had a higher degree of Indian blood, "maintained their legal status as wards of the federal government" and "had limited control over their own financial affairs," while unrestricted citizens "were judged competent to handle their own affairs and were awarded legal independence from federal wardship."[9] Finally, Indian Commissioner Morgan determined during the enrollment process that individual Indians should be renamed if necessary and distributed a circular to that effect.[10]

Thus, the enrollment process established a system that defined who the Chickasaws were, how "Chickasaw" Chickasaws were, how competent Chickasaws were to run their own lives, and what Chickasaws should be named — all this for people who were already considered "civilized."

The period between the passage of the Dawes Act and the termination of the Chickasaw government was a time of tremendous internal strife, just as the period before removal in Mississippi had been. Chickasaws were forced to watch as the federal government dismantled and took control of their nation piece by piece. Although the federal government was actually supposed to take control of the schools with the Curtis Act in 1898, the Chickasaws used every maneuver possible to keep control until 1906, the date of their termination. After statehood, the Bureau of Indian Affairs appointed Chickasaw governors who served as figureheads for their people and as liaisons to the federal government. The governor had limited powers; the Chickasaw legislature was nonexistent.[11] The U.S. government would maintain this policy until 1934, when Congress, under Franklin D. Roosevelt, passed the

Indian Reorganization Act, also known as the Wheeler-Howard Act. The Reorganization Act repealed the allotment system and allowed tribes, at their own option, to "incorporate under provisions of the act and elect tribal governments invested with certain legal powers." [12]

Chickasaws, however, did not elect their own governor until 1973. The first appointed Chickasaw governor in 1906 was none other than Douglas Johnston, the well-respected and well-loved former student and superintendent of Bloomfield Academy. Johnston served as governor until his death in 1939. Bloomfield remained in operation as a boarding academy for girls until 1949. Johnston, during his governorship, may have used his position to help keep the school open. Johnston was not alone; Charles D. Carter, a Chickasaw-Cherokee, was elected to represent Oklahoma's fourth district in the U.S. Congress from 1907–26, a particularly significant accomplishment at that time. Carter had a vested personal interest in the fate of the boarding school. Not only had he been a student of the Chickasaw Manual Labor Academy for Males (Harley), but his father, Benjamin Carter, had served as superintendent from 1882–87. [13] Charles Carter, for whom the school would later be renamed, secured the appropriations for improvements for Bloomfield and worked to keep the school open. Consequently, the Chickasaws may not have had any real power of their own or clout with the federal government, but two of their most respected members did.

Literacy Purposes and Change

For the Chickasaws, literacy instruction through formal schooling was a tradition, and Bloomfield was the symbol of this tradition. During the golden age the Chickasaws controlled Bloomfield and provided literacy instruction for the students that would fulfill their goals as a nation. Students, striving to attain the ideals of True Womanhood, were training to become leaders in their community and in Indian Territory.

The federal government had other purposes. The government used the Dawes and Curtis Acts as weapons to dissolve tribal governments, solving the "Indian problem" once and for all. The government, having granted U.S. citizenship to enrolled Chickasaws, expected tribal members to become good citizens by completely acculturating and believed that Bloomfield, like the off-reservation boarding schools in operation throughout the nation, would be the perfect place to accomplish these goals. Commissioner of Indian Affairs Thomas J. Morgan clarified the goals of the federal government in his instructions to Indian agents and school superintendents in 1889: "The great purpose which the Government has in view in providing an ample system of common school education for all Indian youth of school age, is the preparation of them for American citizenship. The Indians are destined to become absorbed into the national life, not as Indians, but as Americans. . . . [Teachers should] endeavor to awaken reverence for the nation's power, gratitude for its beneficence, pride in its history, and a laudable ambition to contribute to its prosperity." [14]

Morgan's words illustrate that policymakers still strongly believed in the power of literacy to effect fundamental change — they saw literacy instruction through formal schooling as the necessary agent to change patriotic Chickasaw citizens into patriotic U.S. citizens.

Bureau administrators began their period of control by making several significant changes. The first change dealt with the school's administration. Professor E. B. Hinshaw, who had long been a favorite professor, principal, and administrator at Bloomfield, was succeeded by J. R. Hendrix, who was appointed by the government. Hendrix had also served as superintendent of the Ardmore Public Schools. [15] Officials also made two changes in the school's funding. Under both missionary and Chickasaw control, funding had always been provided to allow for a ten-month school year; the federal government provided funds for only a nine-month school year. Furthermore, the ten-dollar monthly payment to families who boarded their children was discontinued. [16] In addition, administrators altered the school's general setup by reducing the grade levels from twelve to eight and then by restoring the ninth grade in 1927. [17] Significantly, they also introduced a new domestic literacy curriculum, training students could put into immediate practice; under federal control, students would take care of the general maintenance of the school.[18] Domestic literacy training was a necessary part of citizenship training, the federal government's objective.

According to Bloomfield superintendent Eleanor Allen, in an interview with educator Ralph Hall in 1933, the mission of the school "was to develop an all-around efficient citizen" by providing instruction in "industry, esthetics, [and] civic and community interests" in addition to basic academic instruction and cultural training. Allen considered the school "a preparatory school in more than one sense."[19] Students were prepared to attend high school at one of the Indian schools, Chilocco Indian School or Haskell Institute, or to attend public high school. Because many students did not continue their education but went back home or married and began homes of their own, a primary focus of the school was to enable the students to make those homes better places by providing training in "home living," that is, domestic art and science, cleaning, gardening, animal care, nutrition, and etiquette. In other words, the students were being taught "how to live" whatever sort of life they chose and to help others in their families and communities. Allen never mentions assimilation as an objective of the school; perhaps, that is because it was so generally accepted as the objective that it need not be said.

A final change dealt with the school's student population. From 1917 to 1929, when the school was maintained with Chickasaw funds, which were controlled by the federal government, the school was open to Chickasaw girls only, of any degree of blood. After 1929, the school was maintained by federal funds and was open to American Indian girls of any tribe who had at least one-quarter or more degree of blood. However, although girls of any tribe were allowed to enroll, the majority of students were Chickasaw and Choctaw. Most of the remaining students were members of one of the other southeastern tribes, Cherokee, Creek, and Seminole. Federal authorities were interested in enrolling "restricted" students, who often had a higher degree of blood, and any students who had the poorest educational advantages at home.[20] Government Indian agents also strongly encouraged orphans and partial orphans to attend.

This system for school enrollment differed greatly from previous systems. Under missionary control, all families were encouraged to send their daughters. Under Chickasaw control, students applied to attend and were selected based on their ability to meet the entrance requirements, one of which was basic literacy. Under federal control, students attended for various reasons. I asked each of the women I interviewed why they had attended Bloomfield Academy or Carter Seminary instead of a public school. The answers varied, to a certain extent according to when they attended. For example, women who attended in the 1910s and 1920s were often sent to Bloomfield because attending the boarding academies was a family tradition. Hettie McCauley King, a student in the 1920s, remembers how proud her parents were to be graduates of Chickasaw boarding schools: "Well, my parents sent me because my mother went to the old Bloomfield . . . and my dad was in a government school . . . I forgot the name of where he went [Harley] . . . she just believed in education. And it was a government school . . . back then . . . it was considered really good."[21] Hettie's remark indicates that her mother, a graduate of Bloomfield under Chickasaw control, "believed in education" and, furthermore, believed in government-run education. Bloomfield had obviously kept its good reputation, even though the Oklahoma public school system had been in place for a number of years.

For Juanita Keel Tate, a student in 1918, attending Bloomfield was not only a matter of tradition but a matter of practicality. She recalled how her mother, a graduate of old Bloomfield, "was determined that we were going to get our education" in spite of the family's financial difficulties. Juanita's mother, Lula Potts Keel, was responsible for raising and educating twelve children. Juanita said that her mother "saw that we were all educated, and that is really the reason we all attended Indian schools. We could get a good education with practically no expense."[22] Like Hettie's mother, Juanita's mother valued education — to such an extent that all twelve of her children attended boarding schools instead of helping out at home.

Some of the women I spoke with remember being influenced by the stories of older sisters, cousins, and aunts who were attending Bloomfield. For example, Frances Griffin Robinson, who attended in 1927–29, remembers pleading to go to Bloomfield after seeing how "different" her cousin Dinah was on her very first visit home. She recalled, "I have a first cousin [Dinah] . . . had a first cousin, and she is Amanda's grandmother. We were practically raised together. But she got to go to Bloomfield because she was orphaned in that her father was not living. When she came home the first time from Bloomfield, she was just so groomed and everything, you know, just so different, and I wanted to go. So I just kept on and kept on until . . . my dad was the one who had the say-so . . . and they took me to Bloomfield." Frances did not think she would get to go because, as she remarked, "They would not just take you if you lived near a school. They'd rather take orphans and children that lived a long way from school." Frances felt lucky because her walk to the nearest public school was difficult, enabling her to attend Bloomfield. She said, "So, let's see, I lived about five or six miles from Bethel School, and we had to, of course, walk, and a lot of times when we would have a heavy, heavy rain — well, it would be hard for us to get across a little old branch. And . . . but this is the only way that helped me get into Bloomfield." [23]

Frances wanted to attend because she wanted to be like her cousin Dinah, who was "so groomed." She actually attended because of her difficulty getting to school. Frances was hardly the only woman who spoke of practicality and the difficulty of getting to a school from rural locations. Many women, especially depression-era students, spoke of hard times and education disadvantages and stated that going to Carter was the only way to get an education. A few remember being recruited by an Indian agent because of their home situations. Fannye Williford Skaggs and Leona Williford Isaac (1933–47) related the following story, which is exemplary of what many depression-era students expressed:

Well, we lived out on a farm and at that time, there was . . . we didn't have a car and the school was probably. . . . Yes, across the creek where you had to have mules to get everyone across when the creek was up. There was no bridge there at that time. . . . This was back in the years of the depression anyway. And there was no money. . . . And some of the people in the neighborhood that were around there that had to go to that school had their feet wrapped up in tow sacks in the winter time. It was not an easy time. . . . You know there was no money, and no food, and no grass, and no water, and no animals. . . . That's why we were sent, I'm sure. Part of it . . . I understood that Indian agent . . . you had to pay if you were Indian and you went to a public school anyway. . . . So . . . but things were different when you had an Indian agent to take care of your business for you, and the business included the children and where they went to school. So I know that my mother . . . I have no doubt what she said when she was advised to send us to boarding school so the Indian Department would not have to pay that school any money. . . . Because whatever that Indian agent advised them to do, they probably did because supposedly it would have been for their benefit.[24]

Fannye and Leona's story not only expresses how difficult life was during the Great Depression years in Oklahoma but also gives insight to the way in which students were recruited by the government and what families' attitudes might have been about Indian agents and the Bureau of Indian Affairs.

Like Fannye and Leona, Mary Pittman Parris, Clara Pittman Gatlin, and Ula Mae Pittman Welch (1935–47) also said that they went to Carter because "the government came to see our mother and said we had to." The Pittman sisters were considered partial orphans because their father died when they were very young, thus making them candidates for recruitment. Mary, Clara, and Ula Mae made the following statement, which not only explains why they had to go but also reflects what they thought about the decision:

There were nine children and our daddy died in 1934 . . . we didn't even get to go home for at least a year or two. . . . I had to go up there when I was six. And I was the youngest. How I missed my mama. But I got over it. And I really . . . We had real good food. Three meals a day. A nice warm bed and clean linen. They taught us to always be clean and to take care of our teeth. They took good care of our health. . . . But I really enjoyed it, and I really appreciated it because it really taught us things. And we had good things that we probably never would have had.[25]

The Pittmans' story is probably typical of the experiences of many women who attended Bloomfield or Carter. Many women spoke of homesickness at first but also realized that they "had good things" — they were well fed, well dressed, warm, and taken care of. Indian agents recruited children from single-parent families or from any family having financial difficulty whose children were at an educational disadvantage. Agents recruited students with educational disadvantages, often from rural, primarily Indian communities and with higher degrees of Indian blood because they wanted to acculturate these students as much as possible, their purpose for literacy education.

Government officials believed that U.S. citizenship training would be effective only if students ceased to be citizens of their Indian nation and gave up the traditions and customs of their cultures. Because of this the school did not emphasize or even expose the students to any aspect of Native history, heritage, or culture. In fact, in 1889, Indian Commissioner Thomas Morgan instructed teachers to teach the students how to be Americans and to "carefully avoid any unnecessary reference to the fact that they are Indians."[26] This policy continued for many years. As Frances Griffin Robinson (1927–29) commented, "We were never exposed [to Chickasaw History]. I sure don't remember any of it. . . . I don't think they . . . I think that they wanted us changed."[27] Fannye Williford Skaggs and Leona Williford Isaac (1933–47) agreed that the school was trying to change them and described the changing process in greater detail. According to Fannye and Leona, "[Teaching Native heritage and history] was not done then. They were taking this Indian person and turning them into . . . a white person. So you have to eliminate everything culturally and everything else to get rid of that Indian, you know. Of course, it doesn't always work, but they tried very hard to do that, you know." [28]

Some students fared better at the school than others. Mary Pittman Parris, Clara Pittman Gatlin, and Ula Mae Pittman Welch (1935–47) spoke of children, usually those of higher degrees of blood, who "couldn't handle it." They observed, "A lot of those little kids could not adjust that were more Indian. . . . We grew up around our non-Indian relatives, so we were never steeped in the Indian tradition. . . . They just tried to get that out of you. They didn't want you to have any . . . They were changing us. . . . You had to change with the times, and that is where a lot of Indians have gone astray because they could not adjust. There are not enough programs to help them to live in what they call 'the white man's world.' " [29]

The Pittmans seem to accept what was happening as "just the way things were then" and also to believe that changing with the times and adjusting to a "white man's world" is necessary. Claudine Williford King (1939–48) made a similar comment. Claudine is extremely proud of her heritage but does not regret what she was taught at Carter. She mentioned that they did learn some Indian history, for example,

We learned the Five Civilized Tribes and where they were located in the state . . . you know the old Picken's district and all those . . . the way the state was divided when they said that the Indians were going to get to have it all . . . you know, from now on. Ha. But they taught us all of that and then . . . it wasn't an emphasis on Indians so much as it was just that they told us how it had been. They went on and taught us about other history. You know . . . the emphasis then, and I think it was good, and I think it should be that way now, was on everybody being American first and something else second, you know. I just think it was better that way . . . it works better that way. [30]

Claudine's statement indicates that she, like the Pittman sisters, thinks that the method the school used was probably the "best way," or a least a way to succeed in life. Although many women said they regretted not learning more about their culture and heritage growing up and took steps to learn more about it in their adulthood, they also believed that changing and adjusting was a necessary part of growing up.

As Leona Williford Isaac said, "So you have to eliminate everything culturally and everything else to get rid of that Indian, you know."[31] The first item on the government's agenda for elimination was the use of native languages. Forbidding the use of native languages was a standard practice at federally run Indian boarding schools throughout the nation and had been since their inception. In 1887, Indian Commissioner J. D. C. Atkins argued for the exclusive use of English in Indian schools on the following grounds:

> the rising generation will be . . . required . . . to fill the measure of citizenship, and the main purpose of educating them is to enable them to read, write, and speak the English language and to transact business with English-speaking people. When they take . . . the responsibilities . . . of citizenship their vernacular will be of no advantage. Only through the medium of the English tongue can they acquire a knowledge of the Constitution of the country. . . . Every nation is jealous of its own language, and no nation ought to be more so than ours, which approaches nearer than any other nationality to the perfect protection of its people. True Americans all feel that the Constitution, laws, and institutions of the United States . . . are superior to those of any other country; and they should understand that by the spread of the English language will these laws and institutions be more firmly established and widely disseminated.[32]

Language, an obvious cultural marker, is one of the most basic aspects of an individual's personal and cultural identity. By forbidding students to speak their native languages, the government was, in effect, forbidding students to participate in their cultures or even communicate with members of their cultures. Teaching literacy in English and only English was one way the government could shape the students' identities so that they would consider themselves Americans and not Chickasaws, Choctaws, or Cherokees.

Of course, as Leona also said, "it doesn't always work." [33] Although government educators can attempt to strip students of what they consider "Indian" characteristics, tribes, who decide their own identities, can define and redefine what it means to be Indian, selecting aspects of American culture and integrating it into their own. Throughout the academy's history, students were strictly forbidden to use their native languages anywhere — in the classroom, on the playground, or in private. Fanny Hughes Bass, a student from 1911 to 1914, stated, "They didn't want anyone to speak Chickasaw . . . just English." [34]

Students in later years remember finding ways to break the rule. For example, Claudine Williford King (1939–48) stated, "[Students spoke Chickasaw] in our rooms and out on the playground. They . . . you weren't supposed to talk in your native language . . . but we did anyway, especially out on the playgrounds, and we were just careful when we were around the teachers not to do it." But, as Claudine later related, not everyone was careful. Many women also remember students who were punished for "talking Indian." Claudine shared the following story describing the lengths to which one of her friends, a full-blood student, would go to speak her language: "I had this one friend . . . she was full-blooded Choctaw and she was just not going to give up on it. She just talked Choctaw just any time she wanted to, and she foamed at the mouth for the whole eight years because they would wash her mouth out with lye soap when you talked Indian. Yeah. She didn't care. That was her language. In fact, she was more comfortable in that. There were several who were, but she was the one that I remember." [35]

Jeanne Liddell Cochran (1929–33) also remembers the language rule and discussed how difficult it was for some full-blood students who did not speak English at all when they first came to school. Jeanne told the following story, which describes what it was like for non-English-speaking full-blood students and how those students were treated by the teachers as well as the other students:

I remember one girl who came after school had started, and I think I was in probably the second or third grade, and she would not go to class . . . she didn't understand what they were trying to tell her because she did not speak English. And she would have been in that class, and so when it was time to go into the classroom, she refused to go, and they asked me to go see if I could coax her into the classroom . . . and she would not go. She would just shake her head, and I don't remember how they finally got her to go to the classroom, but I did feel sorry for her because I felt that it was the fact that she . . . I think she might have known a little bit of English, but the fact that they mostly spoke whatever her language was what made it so hard for her. And, of course, she was frightened to death of being away from home. . . . I think some students knew enough [English] that they could [leave home] . . . just like this girl. I think that she could understand and could speak a little, but would not. And that's the way they were — more comfortable speaking their Indian language than they were English because they spoke a broken . . . what we called a broken English. . . . I remember this girl — when she left there, she could speak just as well as anybody. And how they did that, I'll never know. But they were patient teachers, and I don't remember that they had any special classes. They just more or less taught those students along with the rest, and they picked it up. Now, not all ever gave up their broken way of speaking, but they certainly could communicate, and we did not think anything about it at all.[36]

Although Jeanne describes the teachers as patient with non-English speakers, the academy's rule about language use seems harsh by today's standards. What is surprising, however, is that students frequently faced the same rule at home. Some parents and grandparents, especially if they were mixed-blood or bilingual, not only discouraged their children from speaking their own native language at home but did not allow them to learn it in the first place. Many parents and grandparents thought that learning Chickasaw or another native language was a detriment. They believed that their children would not succeed in school or other aspects of life unless they knew English and knew it well. Mixed-blood families usually spoke English at home either because the white spouse never learned the native language or because the white spouse did not want the family to speak it. Ida Bell Hughes Martin (1920–30), for example, stated, "My mother didn't allow it. My daddy didn't allow it. My mother . . . talked the Chickasaw language. . . . Well, you see, my daddy was white. And we were in a white district, I guess you would say." [37]

Some of the women I spoke with understand their parents' reasoning for not wanting them to learn the language, but they are saddened by the loss of language and wish they had learned it as children. Dorothy Wall Holt (1940–47) remarked, "We didn't learn it, and I'm so sorry that we didn't, because I would love to be able to talk now." [38] Juanita Keel Tate (1918) remembers listening to her father talk. Her father's first language was Chickasaw, and according to Juanita, "He didn't teach us, per se . . . we really learned a lot just by listening to him when other Chickasaws would visit. . . . Of course, we understood, and we could say quite a few words in Chickasaw." [39] In spite of this, Juanita is not a speaker of Chickasaw.

Some families were more adamant than others about the home language rule and did not even allow the children to hear it spoken. Jeanne Liddell Cochran (1929–33) told the following story to describe how language was handled at her home and why:

> We never . . . this family has never spoken anything except English, but we would ask Grandma Keel, because I knew she could speak it. But I never heard my mother, not once, but I'm sure she knew it. And we would say, "Teach us to speak Indian" . . . not "Chickasaw." And they would not do it. But when we would come into the

room a lot of times, we would hear them speaking it. They immediately stopped. They never spoke it in our presence. My grandmother was adamant about not letting us learn that. We learned a few words. We had an uncle who, when we got out of sight, would . . . teach us some words, but we really did not ever speak the language, which I regret. She said the way of the Indian was gone, and we had to learn the way of the white people.[40]

Although not every family was as strict about the language rule as Jeanne's, none of the women I interviewed were taught to speak their native language as children or could speak it now.

In order for federal educators to achieve their chief literacy purpose, creating "all-around efficient citizens," they had to accomplish two tasks: stripping students of the culture and heritage and immersing them in activities that would foster patriotism and a nationalistic spirit. Agents and superintendents were given specific instructions to introduce students to "the elementary principles of the Government under which they live, and with their duties and privileges as citizens." Commissioner Morgan clearly outlined his plan for the "Inculcation of Patriotism" in Indian schools: "On the campus . . . there should be erected a flagstaff, from which should float constantly . . . the American flag. . . . Patriotic songs should be taught to the pupils, and they should sing them frequently. . . . Patriotic selections should be committed and recited publicly, and should constitute a portion of the reading exercises. . . . National holidays . . . should be observed with appropriate exercises. . . . It will also be well to observe the anniversary of . . . the 'Dawes Bill.'"[41]

Morgan's directives, issued in 1889, were implemented throughout Bloomfield's history; however, the nationalistic activities and the objectives on which they were based were similar, if not identical, to activities at public schools throughout the nation. "Patriotic citizenship" was an objective at every school in the nation for whites as well as Indians. For Indian school students, however, the citizenship activities had more immediate and significant implications. Bloomfield and Carter students, aware that they were being "changed," participated in plays or other activities on national holidays and were encouraged to join the Girl Scouts and other civic and community-minded organizations. The students knew that the school was federally controlled and remember learning about the government in civics classes and discussing current events. As Ora Lee Chuculate Woods (1930–36) recalled,

> We had civics, and we had a flagpole in the middle. . . . In the front lawn of the administration building we had a great big fish pond . . . a great big oval fish pond with goldfish in it. And in the middle of the fish pond there was an island, and you could walk out there to the island to the flag pole, and we would raise the flag every morning and bring it down at sundown every day. And it was a big event, and we really did salute the flag and pledge our allegiance. Yes, and we recognized that the government . . . we learned that the government was good and that it was a government school and that it was because of the government that we were there. You know, we were aware.[42]

Historical circumstances helped the school achieve the federal government's objective of citizenship. Many of the women with whom I spoke attended school during World War I, the Great Depression, or World War II. Depression-era students knew that the government was helping their families; many of their fathers took jobs with the Works Progress Administration WPA, jobs that kept their families from starving. Many students in school during the war years were personally affected by what was going on and wanted to participate in the war effort in some way. Nationalism surged, and according to Juanita Keel Tate (1918), Bloomfield students, patriotic and eager to do their duty, contributed in a number of ways. She recalled, "in my class we knitted dish rags for World War I. They were approximately a foot square. . . . It so happened later on I knitted a sweater for World War II. I said, 'Well I knitted for two wars.' That was good training for us."[43] Other students at Carter throughout World War II, like Dorothy Wall Holt (1940–47), remember growing victory gardens or packing medical kits. She said, "We . . . knit scarves and . . . even packed medical kits . . . for the men."[44]

The women remember the war years vividly, and any discussions of citizenship training almost always turned to memories of war. Students who attended during World War I and II had fathers, brothers, cousins, and uncles fighting overseas and recall worrying about them constantly. Dorothy Wall Holt (1940–47) related the following story: "we had drills . . . blackout drills. We had to cover the windows with blankets . . . that is one thing about Indian men. [Some of the girls had fathers in the war.] A lot . . . most . . . I know in my family, all of them were gone. All that were of age was gone to the war. I had three uncles in the war and some brothers and several cousins. They were all gone except the old men and the little boys."[45]

Juanita Keel Tate's (1918) most striking memory is of Armistice Day. Her description of the students' reactions demonstrates how the war directly and often devastatingly impacted the girls' lives. She commented:

> All I knew is that I had two brothers in World War I, and they were in the army. Ruddy and Overton were both in army camps. So the day that the armistice was signed, Miss Allen . . . called an assembly. . . . I never will forget when Miss Allen . . . stepped up to the podium and announced, "Girls, the war is over. Armistice has been signed." And when she said that, the girls all just whooped and hollered and some just screamed. Others just sat down and cried. One of my cousins, Phelia Lavers, who was sitting right by me, began to sob and she said, "Well, I'm glad the war is over, but it is too late for my brother. He has already been killed in France." . . . Miss Allen herself began to cry, and she said, "Well, there's no reason to say anything further. We're all too full." . . . There was just utter chaos in the room by then. So, she dismissed us. . . . I hugged and held Phelia's hand all the way back to class.[46]

Clara Pittman Gatlin, Mary Pittman Parris, and Ula Mae Pittman Welch (1935–47) shared a similar story. They, too, remembered how they felt at the end of the war, this time, World War II. The Pittman sisters were among those students whose families were hit the hardest by the war. They recalled, "World War II started in '41, and we were there at school . . . our youngest brother got killed. So the war . . . I mean, we don't like to think about the war. . . . one time we had to practice putting on these big old gas masks. I thought boy, it's going to get bad, and they're going to come over here . . . they took us down to . . . that auditorium . . . and we saw the filming of when they dropped the atomic bomb over there. . . . But that ended the war, and we were so happy."[47]

The stories of Dorothy, Juanita, Clara, Mary, and Ula Mae poignantly remind us of the impressive service record of Indian men. American Indians have served in every war American has ever fought and, furthermore, have one of the most distinguished armed services records of any group in American society.[48] Many Indians were granted citizenship with the implementation of the Dawes Act; however, many were not. As a matter of fact, American Indian soldiers in World War I were not made citizens until *after* the war, in 1919, when Congress passed an act stipulating that Indians who served in the military during World War I could be granted citizenship at their request. It was not until 1924 that Congress passed the Indian Citizenship Act, which granted citizenship to any American Indian who had not yet received it.[49]

These statistics highlight the complexity of the concepts of citizenship and patriotism for American Indian people and the complexity of their feeling about being "American." Indians, U.S. citizens or not, have faithfully served the United States. The women I interviewed all very much view themselves as "Americans." They also view themselves as "Chickasaws" and more collectively as "Indians." These are not mutually exclusive identities but are very much intertwined.

Students maintained their tribal identities in spite of the efforts of Bureau of Indian Affairs administrators. In an effort to shape and mold Bloomfield and Carter students, administrators encouraged or required participation in activities designed to foster nationalism and patriotism while at the same time discouraging or forbidding participation in traditional cultural activities. In the 1800s, missionaries built boarding schools far from Indian communities so students would be "far from heathen influences." Students at Bloomfield and Carter, however, were not very far from their families even though they may not have gotten to see them very often.

Although the administration wanted and needed parental and community support, they also needed a method of controlling the students' communication with their families. Letter writing was the chosen method. Pauline Williford Adkins (1932–41) remembers, "We were required to write letters . . . and they read those letters." [50] Frances Griffin Robinson (1927–29), who attended the school much earlier than Pauline, remembers the same practices: "[Letters] were all censored. And if you put anything in there like 'I don't like school' or something about one of your teachers, they would make you do it over. And they read all . . . outgoing and incoming mail. It was all censored." [51]

Letters may have been censored for a number of reasons. Perhaps administrators did not want students to become homesick or complain about the school. Another possible reason is that they wanted to make sure the students were writing in English. Jeanne Liddell Cochran recalls, "We had to write. Everything had to be in English. Everything was English. Indian was out. We were Indian people, but this was a white method." [52] A few women do not remember writing original letters but remember copying letters off the chalkboard in their English classes. Mary Pittman Parris, Clara Pittman Gatlin, and Ula Mae Pittman Welch, who attended Carter during the late 1930s and the 1940s, said, "We had to write once a month. . . . I remember we would say, 'Dear Folks, How are you? Fine, I hope.' All of us wrote the same thing when we wrote. . . . She wrote it on the board. We copied it. I can still see it. 'Dear Folks.' And I use to think, 'What are folks?' And 'How are you?' And the government saw that we mailed the letters. And they were free." [53]

Letter writing and censorship, citizenship training, and student population are a few of the significant ways the federal government changed

Bloomfield after taking control in 1906. Chickasaws did not seem to mind these changes in the school's later years — that was just the way things were. Bloomfield, or later Carter, was considered a good school, and many students, for various reasons, felt lucky to be able to attend. However, Chickasaws did mind the changes in the school made immediately after the federal takeover; many families made their feelings known.

Chickasaws had always been proud of their school system, and Bloomfield, particularly, was a symbol of all they had accomplished. After the federal government terminated the Chickasaw government and shut down nearly all of their schools, Chickasaws were upset and found a way to retaliate. Under missionary and tribal control, Chickasaw families showed their support by sending their daughters to school and keeping Bloomfield's enrollment at capacity. The obvious way for Chickasaw families to show their opposition to federal control, then, was to refuse to send their daughters, which is exactly what many did. Under tribal control the school's enrollment averaged 115, with an average attendance of 100; under the first year of federal control, 1907–08, the school's enrollment totaled only 43, with a poor average attendance of 24. Enrollment dropped severely at Bloomfield for the next few years, plunging so low that, according to the 1911 annual report, Bloomfield maintained an average attendance of only 65 percent, the lowest average attendance of any federally operated Indian boarding school.[54]

The Chickasaw's opposition of the school did not begin to lessen until 1910, when Annie Ream Addington, a member of the much respected Guy family of the Chickasaw Nation, took over the superintendentship of Bloomfield. As opposition continued to decrease, enrollments increased, and several improvements were made to the buildings, including the addition of cottages for domestic training.[55] Addington's administration continued until January 24, 1914, when fire completely destroyed the school and all of its records.[56] Bloomfield was not rebuilt, but was instead relocated to the site of the old Hargrove College in Ardmore, Oklahoma.

Because the Hargrove buildings required many improvements and repairs, Bloomfield did not reopen until 1917. Much to the dissatisfaction of Chickasaw people, the school was completely maintained by Chickasaw funds, which were controlled by the Department of Interior, from 1917 to 1929. Appropriations for the school from federal funds did not begin until 1930.[57] The school opened under the administration of one of the school's best known superintendents, Eleanor Allen. Allen, who had previously served as superintendent of the Wheelock Academy, a fact that probably comforted many Chickasaw families, is known for the many improvements made to Bloomfield during her administration, including the laying of the sewer, water, and gas lines and the addition of two wings to the Academic Building. In addition, she added a heating plant and steam laundry with equipment, a dormitory, which had a dining room, kitchen, bakery, and home economics department, and a dairy barn and cattle. She also improved the landscaping of the campus by adding many trees, a goldfish pool and flag pole, a small lake and outdoor stage, and works of art inside the buildings.[58]

Allen's administration continued until her first retirement in 1921, when she was succeeded by Minta Foreman, the superintendent at Wheelock Academy.[59] Allen returned in 1923 and made several other improvements including a small cottage, poultry house, mule barn, oil house, boiler house, commissary, garage and implement shed, and employees' club.[60] Eleanor Allen remained until her second retirement in 1934.[61] During Allen's administration in 1932, the school was renamed Carter Seminary in honor of Charles Carter, who had always championed the school. Allen was the school's best known and perhaps most influential administrator. Very little information about the school's other superintendents or teachers exists.

The teachers at the academy under federal control were employed by the U.S. Civil Service and were required to meet civil service standards. According to the Bloomfield Seminary Edition of the *Oklahoma Indian Magazine* in 1932, "Higher qualifications are now required for entrance to civil service teaching positions and together with the appointment of a special supervisor for the elementary grades, the standard of instruction is being rapidly raised."[62] At the time of Ralph Hall's interviews with Eleanor Allen in 1933, the Bloomfield staff consisted of "a clerk, five academic teachers, music teacher, two home economic teachers, two matrons, assistant matron, cook, laundress, physician, engineer, dairyman, laborer, and two students assistants." The teachers were paid year round and had thirty days of annual leave and thirty days of compulsory educational leave, during which time teachers worked toward credit hours for higher degrees.[63] Unlike the teachers under missionary and Chickasaw control, who were frequently graduates of eastern women's colleges, teachers under federal control came from around the area.

Most of the women remembered very little background information about their teachers, if they were ever told any in the first place, and the names of teachers were long forgotten, with the exception of a few favorites. Many women recalled that the majority of their teachers were white women. According to Dorothy Wall Holt (1940–47), "A lot of our teachers were Caucasian. If they were Indian, they weren't identifiable. If you looked at them, you would say they weren't Indian."[64] Jeanne Liddell Cochran (1929–33) does not remember any "visible" Indian teachers either. She commented, "I don't recall that they were Indian . . . they were fair . . . I just assumed that they were not Indian. . . . And I do not know what the qualifications had to be in order to get a job there, but it was really . . . I would think at that time, a choice place for teaching."[65] Native teachers seem to have been few and far between, but not entirely absent, especially in the later years. A few women specifically remember Indian teachers. Fannye Williford Skaggs and Leona Williford Isaac (1933–47) recalled, "We had a full-blooded Navajo Indian woman that taught arts and crafts. . . . She also taught at Chilocco because she was there when I went freshman year. She was teaching weaving."[66] Claudine Williford King (1939–48), on the other hand, remembers otherwise. She commented, "We had several Indian teachers, and my second-grade teacher was a graduate of Chilocco."[67] Pauline Williford Adkins, a student in the 1930s, also remembers Native teachers and staff. She remarked, "Most of them were white. . . . We did have one lady that was Indian that I can remember . . . well, we had two. We had a Miss Lambert that came from Dougherty. And then we had this Canadian . . . she was Indian and French but came from Canada . . . Miss Hudson. And she wasn't there very long before Van Noy [Hughes] replaced her, and Van Noy, I guess, was [Chickasaw]." [68]

Although Bloomfield and Carter may not have recruited Native teachers frequently, the fact that a few were employed is significant. One of Bloomfield's earliest teachers under missionary control was Serena Factor, a full-blood and Bloomfield graduate. The Van Noy mentioned by Pauline is Van Noy Hughes, also a graduate of Bloomfield. Many women remember "Aunt Noy" because of the long years that she worked at Bloomfield and Carter and because of her dedication to the school and her students. Van Noy was mentioned by several women as an important role model, not just because she was Indian, but because she was from the same region and was raised in similar circumstances, and because she and her sisters also attended Bloomfield. Van Noy was someone who understood.

Van Noy was not the only role model. All of the teachers, among their other duties, served as role models, showing the students how to be "ladies." The teachers may have been the first formally educated women whom many students knew or with whom they had relationships, and they helped instill a strong belief in education in many women. A few of the women remember specific teachers because of the special relationship they had with them. Ora Lee Chuculate Woods (1930–36), for example, described one teacher, Miss Brigman, as a major influence in her life and even expressed that her relationship with Miss Brigman was what she valued the most about her education at Bloomfield. In the following story she explains why:

[My relationship] with Miss Brigman, for instance, the music teacher. I value that more than anything because I think she really made a difference to me . . . because she opened up so many possibilities, because we listened to good music, and because we understood that it's more than what we can do, it's that we can appreciate what others can do. And it was just wonderful, and she was just a wonderful person — she was. [She showed me that there was] something we could grow to. And she was just really a challenge, and I really did admire her. She really did help me.[69]

Clara Pittman Gatlin, Mary Pittman Parris, and Ula Mae Pittman Welch (1935–47) were very impressed with their teachers; some teachers were special — maybe because they were "real ladies" and were friendly or pretty or mannerly. The teachers that had the greatest influence seemed to treat the students courteously and with respect. The students respected these teachers and sought their validation. Clara, Mary, and Ula Mae remembered one teacher in particular who had quite an influence on them:

They got the best teachers. . . . We had Miss Gormley, remember her? And we thought she was so pretty, and she took a screen test, and it wouldn't take. She was too pretty for the movies. And she was part Cherokee . . . and friendly . . . when we got into the classroom, we all behaved ourselves. . . . And all of the teachers dressed real neat, and they were mannerly and all, and they were trying to make ladies out us. . . . They taught us how to have little tea parties . . . we had our little tea cups, and I spilled mine one time and that embarrassed me. . . . I remember we would be looking at her [Miss Gormley], and she would say, "Why are you girls looking at me?" And we would say, "Because you are so pretty." And she was.[70]

All of the women with whom I spoke expressed satisfaction with their teachers and believe that they were well trained to do their jobs. Juanita Keel Tate, who lived in Ardmore her entire life, remarked, "Even in associating with some of the teachers like the last thirty or forty years . . . They were very dedicated people . . . and they sincerely wanted to turn out good students, and they made an effort to really understand those Indian students."[71]

The Curriculum of Citizenship

The teachers under federal control, like the teachers under missionary and Chickasaw control, had many duties besides teaching. Teachers were expected to organize and advise various student activities and clubs, take students on field trips, and generally serve as role models, ladies with "high moral standards" whom the girls were meant to emulate. Maintaining high moral standards was considered part of becoming "a well-rounded individual," one of the chief objectives of the school; consequently, the school did provide religious literacy instruction.

While religious literacy training was definitely a part of life at Bloomfield and Carter, it was not as heavily emphasized as it was during the period of missionary control. However, providing a Christian atmosphere was considered essential to the girls' training and was even thought of as a "Bloomfield tradition." The *Oklahoma Indian School Magazine* states, "A well organized Sunday school and two large religious societies meet regularly every Sunday. A high moral standard is one of the chief objectives of the school. . . . A Christian atmosphere pervades the life at the school which we like to think an emanation of the spirit of its founders." [72] Juanita Keel Tate remembers specific religious assignments and how she felt when she accomplished them. She recalls one example in particular: "Once at Sunday school she asked us to learn the names of the books of the Bible by the next Sunday and those that did would be rewarded . . . so I worked all week. . . . I will never forget that . . . I worked all week and the next week I was the only one in class who actually knew the name of every book in the Bible. I was so proud. I don't remember what the reward was and I didn't care, but I was so happy to know that." [73]

Although the school was originally run by the Methodist-Episcopal Church, no particular denomination took precedence over religious literacy training under either Chickasaw or government control. Only a few women recall occasionally attending church services on campus; instead, others recall being taken to a variety of different churches in Ardmore. For example, according to Pauline Williford Adkins (1932 –

41), "A different preacher would come out and speak, and then we had our choir. . . . I was in the choir there at one time, and we use to sing at the Episcopal Church. . . . But the girls that wanted to go to church on Sundays could go, and they didn't go to the same one every Sunday. They would go to different churches. Maybe the First Baptist one Sunday, Presbyterian the next and something like that."[74]

Religious literacy instruction was never as heavily emphasized as it was under missionary control, but it was an important part of the curriculum under every administration. Academic literacy instruction, on the other hand, was always the most basic part of the curriculum under every administration; however, it was never the most important or the most heavily emphasized under any administration.

Under Chickasaw control the academic literacy curriculum, which was considered equal to a junior college education, was impressive, but the exceptional social literacy curriculum overshadowed this academic literacy curriculum. Oklahoma statehood led to the development of the state public school system. When the federal government took control of Bloomfield, administrators standardized the curriculum, changing the academic literacy curriculum at Bloomfield in accordance with state standards and appointed J. R. Hendrix as the superintendent of Bloomfield. Hendrix was chosen because he also served as the superintendent of the Ardmore Public Schools and could help implement the standardized curriculum. According to the 1932 "Bloomfield Seminary Edition" of *Oklahoma Indian School Magazine*, the students used the state textbooks and followed the Oklahoma Course of Study. Approximately a third of the students' time was spent on academic subjects; the remaining time was devoted to domestic literacy instruction and recreational activities.[75] Although this magazine does not list any specific subjects, my grandmother, Ida Mae (Dinah) Pratt Cobb's report card, issued in 1926, lists grades for the following academic subjects: agriculture, arithmetic, civics, current events, English, penmanship, reading, history, and spelling. Other academic subjects for which no grades are listed include algebra, botany, chemistry, general science, geography, literary society, physics, and physiology and hygiene. All of the women I talked with considered the academic curriculum at Bloomfield and Carter more than adequate. In fact, Claudine Williford King (1939–48) remarked, "The first year that I went to Chilocco, they tested us as freshmen upon arrival there. There were five or six of us from Carter Seminary in the freshman class, and we were at the top of the charts on all of the tests, and I tested second-year college level when I entered as a freshman at Chilocco. Yeah, that was Carter Seminary. It was a very good education." [76]

Although many women remembered feeling well prepared for high school, few could remember what occurred in their classes. The women tended to remember the most information about their favorite subject or their least favorite subject, or whatever assignment seemed to be the most demanding at the time. Some women recall specific exercises and activities such as sentence diagramming, math drills, or poetry memorization. Claudine Williford King (1939–48), who excelled in academics both at Carter and Chilocco, remembered what happened in her classes more than anyone else. According to Claudine, "[Memorization] was a constant thing throughout schooling . . . you had to memorize [poems] . . . then everybody had to take their turn and get up and recite them . . . 'The Highwayman' . . . Edna St. Vincent Millay." Claudine was not the only one who remembered having to memorize poetry. A few can even still recite the poems. Nearly every woman recalled being encouraged to read books. Claudine remembered that teachers "would encourage you to go [to the library] and they would keep track of how many books you read — in one of the later grades . . . fourth or fifth grade, I read sixty books. I remember getting some kind of star for that. But that was not unusual. There . . . everybody read. They were expected to read. . . . They encouraged us to read any kind of book that was in the library. And many of them . . . looking back on it, were, I think, probably ahead of the grade levels that they had there." [77]

Claudine also remembers that teachers heavily emphasized writing skills, not just penmanship. She recalled, "We had to do a written report of several pages. . . . You had to have more than one page of a written book report or . . . essays. . . . You wrote about what you did during the summer [and] Christmas." And, of course, most students remember spending plenty of time at the blackboard diagramming or "parsing" sentences. What Claudine found equally important, however, was the emphasis on developing public speaking skills. "You not only had to write these things, but you had to begin getting up in front of the class — and there were no exceptions . . . and giving oral book reports once a month, or oral presentations of some kind, so that you became equally able to express your thoughts as well as write them." [78]

Jeanne Liddell Cochran (1929–33) also remembered the special attention to oral presentations, correct grammar, and diction. An emphasis on using the English language, both spoken and written, and using it well was ever present. She explained, "We did have to learn proper diction. We could not say 'git.' We couldn't say . . . we always had to say 'singing,' 'thinking' . . . 'ing' . . . 'ing,' you know. They drilled us on that constantly. I think that they stressed that [correct grammar] more than other subjects. However, you spent equal time on everything." [79] Claudine and Jeanne's accounts of academic classes and work demonstrate that learning English literacy — that is, reading, writing, and speaking — was an important part of the academic literacy curriculum and that learning to write and speak in the officially sanctioned manner was crucial.

The academic literacy curriculum at Bloomfield and Carter was equal to the curriculum of the Ardmore Public Schools. The academy had a good reputation in the Ardmore community, not only because of its academic standards, but also because of the number of extracurricular activities provided. Under Chickasaw control, social literacy instruction was the most heavily emphasized strand of the curriculum. The students achieved excellence in the fine and performing arts, and the high number of cultural events Bloomfield offered served as the basis for the school's prestigious reputation as the "Bryn Mawr of the West."

This tradition continued under federal control; the social literacy curriculum was very well developed. Classes in art appreciation were given, and classes in music were held four days a week, with extra choir practices. [80] Fannye Williford Skaggs and Leona Williford Isaac (1933–47) remembered choir practices and special performances: "We sang the

'Hallelujah Chorus' . . . and also . . . we went down and sang at the radio station, and it was recorded at Ardmore . . . KVSO . . . and we recorded Indian chants."[81] Many girls were given instruction in certain instruments in addition to their vocal training. The instruments taught depended on who the music teacher was at the time. Pauline Williford Adkins (1932–41) remembered playing in the school orchestra. According to Pauline, "They had pianos all over that school. I imagine that there were six or eight or more in the administration building. They taught piano lessons. . . . I started violin lessons. There were some that played clarinet or the violins and cello and the bass viola and the piano."[82]

Major plays were held once a year at the outdoor stage and included such plays as "Shakespeare's Midsummer Night's Dream, and operettas such as Hansel and Gretel, and Pandora, or the Paradise of Children."[83] Holiday plays were always a favorite. Everyone remembered taking part in a Thanksgiving play. Ula Mae Pittman Welch (1940–47) laughed as she recounted, "We had one about the pilgrims, Indians and pilgrims, and one year I was Indian."[84] Fannye Williford Skaggs and Leona Williford Isaac (1933–47) remembered how elaborate the dramatic productions were:

We had a little room in the back behind the stage that was filled full of every kind of costume you could imagine. So if you put on a cowboy show, you had everything that went with it. If you put on a George Washington, you had everything that went with it — the dress, the shoes, the buckles, the wigs. . . . And also too, you didn't just have costumes, they had backdrops that just rolled down off the stage that came down to set the scene, so to speak. . . . Yes, when Thanksgiving came along, we had everything but the turkey. . . . The costumes, the hats, the buckles on the shoes . . . I remember doing the Highland Fling and the [costume] was plaid you know with the little black hat . . . and oh, yes, I was on the end and got slung for . . . oh, yes. I recall Mrs. Brigman was very, very precise and very determined that everything was going to be right.

So every step, every song, every move you made was . . . she was a good teacher.[85]

Many women recall specific recitations, musical events, plays, costumes, and dances, events that broke the monotony of academic classes and domestic detail and became the highlights of their school careers. A few women's favorite memories are of their participation in "programs," weekly events that Jeanne Liddell Cochran (1929–33) explains:

> We had what we called a "program," they called it an "assembly," once a week. And one of the teachers presented the program. And I learned poetry, so I was called on by the other teachers to recite poetry during the program. And sometimes they would have a play. Sometimes it would be a dance, like a certain dance of a certain country. See, we learned all of those things . . . at the time you were learning to do the dances, you learned the history of all of this. You know, everything was made into a learning process. You didn't just get out there . . . it was fun, but you learned what went behind these dances and the costumes and things that you wore. . . . I remember that I had to memorize the whole book of Hiawatha. They called it "Heawatha."[86]

According to the *Oklahoma Indian School Magazine*, "The special programs through the year are given much thought and preparation to the end that no child is conscious of having failed in her part."[87] The women vividly remember their participation in programs and plays; some can still remember their stage fright. Their memorabilia and pictures frequently consist of programs or pictures of themselves in costumes performing everything from the minuet to the Highland fling. They all remembered performing, not just for their parents, but more often for social clubs in the Ardmore community. Performing was a part of life at Bloomfield and Carter.

Social literacy instruction was definitely an important part of the school's curriculum. The social literacy curriculum served to introduce the students to the type of culture valued in American society through specific poetry, books, music, art, plays, and dances. However, Bureau of Indian Affairs administrators used the social literacy curriculum for different purposes than the Chickasaws had during their period of control. Chickasaw leaders wanted to train their daughters to be socially refined ladies who were capable of leadership in both Chickasaw and white communities, women who could help them compete in a white world. For federal educators, social literacy training was a way to steep students in western culture and tradition. Social, academic, and religious literacy instruction all contributed to the making of "well-rounded" individuals and good, solid U.S. citizens.

The final type of literacy curriculum, domestic, would not only make the students well-rounded but would prepare them for the type of life the federal government expected them to lead — a life of homemaking. Teaching homemaking skills in school had become a national trend; home economic classes, domestic art and science, were staples of public schools everywhere. Bloomfield and Carter students received the same sort of domestic literacy training that public school students received. Students were required to take six hours a week of instruction and laboratory work in domestic science, cooking, and six hours of domestic art, sewing.[88] Many women remember domestic art and science classes as their favorite subjects. In the following account, Frances Griffin Robinson, a student in the 1920s, describes her first experiences learning to sew:

> Domestic science was our cooking, and domestic art was the sewing. Now I really enjoyed those classes. Made good grades . . . we had them every day. The best I can remember . . . when I first started hemstitching, she let us do a tea towel first . . . mine was just black, because I would have to take it out so much. And the others, too. Our little old hands, I guess, were dirty. I don't know how they could be as strict as they were on us but we just . . . I just practically wore my hem out just trying. . . . So I wish I could have had that. I don't know what they did with it. But I sure still know all of those first things that we did like hemstitching, backstitch-

ing, and all of that, you know. I learned how to embroidery. But I enjoyed those two classes, and the teachers were real nice to us, but they wanted us to do it right . . . just that one way.[89]

The Pittman sisters (1940–47) also talked about the sewing classes and remembered particular projects. Ula Mae noted how advanced they were in comparison to classes at public schools. She related the following story that proves what good seamstresses they became: "Our sewing had to be just so. In fact, I came back here my sophomore year and went to . . . high school here in Durant, and I was in the tenth grade and they had sewing, and they put me with the seniors, and the dress that I made, they put it on display there. And the teacher told me that I could sew better than the senior girls. But that was due from the sixth to the tenth."[90]

However, unlike public school students, Bloomfield and Carter students immediately put their skills to use by performing "details," helping with the school's maintenance in the main kitchen and dining room, as well as in the laundry.[91] Although using student labor was a common practice at off-reservation Indian boarding schools, the period of federal control marked the first time in the history of Bloomfield and Carter that students performed general maintenance tasks instead of hired employees. Government officials believed that the method was cost-efficient and provided good life training for students. The heavy emphasis on domestic literacy training was not lost on the women with whom I spoke. According to the Pittman sisters (1940–47), "It was really a Home Economical school. They were teaching you how to live. Not so much business-like, but in your home."[92]

Other vocational subjects included gardening, animals, basketry (which focused on the making of small furniture and the caning of chairs), leather craft, pottery, and weaving. The leather, pottery, and weaving classes made use of Native American art in their designs.[93] The school employed a Navajo weaver at one point who taught the students how to make Navajo rugs and blankets, which were displayed at the school.

Much time was devoted to homemaking courses and activities. According to the *Oklahoma Indian School Magazine*, "The school endeavors to familiarize the pupils with all the material things that go to make up a well regulated home — chickens, hogs, cows, garden, orchard, flowers, and trees without, and with as much of the useful and beautiful within the home as is possible."[94] As a matter of fact, students received school credit for completing domestic tasks at home in the summers. In a letter to parents written in 1919, Eleanor Allen listed domestic chores for which students could receive school credit. According to the letter, work the students did over the summer would be displayed during the first week of school, and a "credit day program" would be arranged, which Allen encouraged mothers to attend:

> All mothers of our girls will go down on record as members of the Bloomfield Mothers Club, organized in 1919, whether present on that day or not. Encouraging your girls to make the most of what they have learned in school while at home and helping them continue their interest in education during the summer will go far to make the home and school one in bringing our girls up to the high standard of womanhood that all good mothers and teachers desire. Trusting that your children have lightened your cares during the summer and that they have made sunshine in the homes as they did at Bloomfield, I wish to remain with kind regards to you and your family.[95]

This letter demonstrates the stress placed on domestic literacy instruction and enlists the support of the students' mothers so that domestic training would be consistent year round. So much time was devoted to domestic literacy instruction that many women who could not recall the name of a book they read or a play they acted in could recall specific details of their domestic literacy training, especially a garment sewn or re-sewn or a soufflé that failed. Some women remember sewing and cooking instruction as their favorite time of day. Others did not enjoy it at the time but certainly found it useful later in life. As

Claudine Williford King (1939–48) said, "They taught us all of the things that we would need to know to get by." [96]

Detail assignments or school maintenance chores were not considered a part of the domestic curriculum per se but seemed to be the most significant part of domestic instruction; this was the time when instruction was put into real practice. Students performed all of the necessary tasks to keep the school maintained, from cleaning to laundering to keeping animals to gardening. Detail assignments rotated every six to ten weeks so that each student could gain expertise at each task. Regular classes met five days a week; detail had to be done every day. Although some details were more desirable than others, complaining was not an option. No one was exempt. According to Fannye Williford Skaggs and Leona Williford Isaac (1933–47), "Everything was done by the students when I went there. You had no housekeeper that mopped your floor, or made your bed. You did that. They didn't wash your clothes. You did that. . . . You didn't have anyone . . . you did it all. You know you mopped the floors, you waxed, you polished the woodwork, and washed and all of it. It was detail work, and you were assigned to a certain area for so long a time." [97]

In addition to housekeeping chores, detail assignments included helping in the laundry and kitchen and serving in the dining room. No woman said that she actually enjoyed detail, but a few recalled how they made the best of it. The Pittman sisters (1940–47) recounted, "We made a game of the work jobs. Everything that we did, we made a game. We tried to beat each other, but you had to beat them and do it good because they inspected your job. And if it wasn't good, you did it over." [98]

Ula Mae, in particular, remembered a way she had made the most of her detail. She laughed as she shared the following story: "I remember working in the kitchen, and I had to pour the milk. We had the big . . . milk cans. . . . And I . . . was supposed to stir the cream up, but I wouldn't. I would take the cream and pour it in one pitcher and put it on my table. I think that's why I'm so big now," she joked. [99] As Ula

Mae's story points out, students with a sense of humor and spirit adjusted fairly well to the school's detail system and boarding school life in general.

Most of the students from rural areas and farms found the work no different or perhaps easier than what was expected of them at home. Many women expressed pride in their labor and were horrified by the "run-down" state of the school in later years, so different from the shining hallways they remembered. Others remember making the work into games and competition. Some recall the detail assignment they always wanted or the one they were stuck with for too long. Several women commented that they found the domestic literacy instruction useful. According to the Pittman sisters (1940–47), "I really . . . I think that it really helped us. Taught us how to take care of, you know, hygiene, and then go home. . . . Ula made curtains for the house. She always was a good seamstress, and we cleaned the house. You know, we didn't have much, but it taught us, and we helped mama." [100] Many women expressed, like the Pittmans, that they could go home in the summers and help in ways they had been unable to before; they felt like they were really making a difference there.

Old Bloomfield, under Chickasaw control, was known for its ladylike students, the Bloomfield Blossoms. During that time period, the emphasis on manners and etiquette was a part of the social literacy curriculum in which the ideals of True Womanhood were manifested. Under federal control, manners and etiquette were emphasized along with hygiene, health, and child care, making them part of the domestic literacy curriculum. Because of the stress on manners, hygiene, and presenting yourself generally, some women referred to Bloomfield and Carter as a finishing school. Frances Griffin Robinson (1927–29) remembers how particular the teachers and matrons were about manners: "And, gee, our manners had to be just so-so. They told us that . . . it was a finishing school more for ladies." [101] Jeanne Liddell Cochran (1929–33) was also told at Bloomfield that the school was a finishing school. In the following passage, she describes the deportment training: "We had a dining room matron who quietly walked from table to table to teach us our manners . . . very quietly. If she saw you doing something wrong, she would very quietly correct you and tell you why . . . she was very gentle and very quietly correcting our manners all of the time. . . . That school was just like . . . a finishing school because they certainly worked at teaching you what you had to know . . . your manners, your way of presenting yourself . . . all of that. You got that." [102]

Although others do remember being taught etiquette and manners, they did not refer to Bloomfield or Carter as a finishing school. Instead they called it a place where you learned "home living." According to Pauline Williford Adkins (1932–41),

That is one thing that they did teach us — manners and everything like that. That is one thing that I appreciated about the Indian school and of course a lot of the kids today . . . don't get it at home. . . . You know, we learned like table settings and everything like that, where the fork went and all this stuff, and they did teach you things like that . . . like how to set a table. But they did teach us, as I said, manners and keeping yourself clean and everything like that. . . . They tried to teach . . . some of the kids that came into school, I guess, lived so far back out in the woods and everything, and of course we lived out in the woods, too, but we did keep clean even if it was a number two tub and everything, but some of them came to school and they just [didn't] have it. [103]

The emphasis on domestic literacy instruction, both domestic art and science and detail, is evident in a 1928 commencement program, which invites the audience to inspect the work of the students and visit the dormitories and laundry facilities. Demonstrations in the "Home Preservation of Eggs," "Scoring a Dress," and "First Aid" are also items on the program, items noticeably absent from the 1904 program.

BLOOMFIELD
1928
Friday, June First

———

A. PHYSICAL TRAINING
Nine o'clock — On the Campus

———

B. INSPECTION
From ten to eleven
Work of the pupils will be found in the various school rooms.
Guests are also invited to visit the dormitories, laundry, and
premises generally.

———

C. MORNING PROGRAM
Auditorium — From eleven to twelve

First Stanza of our National Anthem .... Audience

Chorus — Greeting to Spring............................. Strauss

Readings —
What is so Rare as a Day in June? .... Lowell
Sophia Frye Reeder
Knee Deep in June .... Riley
Jewel Crummey

Piano Duet —
a. After School March................................. Brownfield
b. Merry Springtime .... Brownfield
Julia Reeder   Theda Goldsby

Demonstrations —
Home Preservation of Eggs .... Willie Turner
Scoring a Dress .... Leslie Morris

Assisted by Julia Reeder

First Aid .... Lourena Hayward

Rhythm Band —

a. Rustic Dance .... Howell

b. Rendezvous .... Komask

Primary Pupils

Readings —

Daisies................................... Frank Demster Sherman

Neva Kirkwood

Little Birdie .... Alfred Tennyson

Pauline Elam

To a Honey Bee .... Alice Carey

Maisie Brown

Prince Tatters .... Laura E. Richards

Aline Hayward

Folk Dances —

Tarantella:

Thelma Steel, Fannie Ned, Leslie Morris,
Catherine McElroy, Winona Setliff, Ursula
Bohreer, Willie Post, Alma McCoy

Highland Fling:

Irma Worcester, Doris Overton, Verna Williford,
Zila Pickens

Piano —

a. Minuet A La' Antique............................. Paderewski

b. Valse Caprice.. Newland

Eva May Price

Vocal Solos —

a. From the Land of the Sky-Blue Water................. Cadman

b. I Love a Little Cottage .... O'Hara

Grace Elam

Exit March — Stars and Stripes Forever.................... Sousa

Dinner
From one to two
Admission by Ticket

Evening Program
Friday, June First
Eight-Thirty
Out-of-door Stage

Play
Midsummer Night's Dream Shakespeare[104]

Commencement under federal control remained the event it had been throughout the school's history, demonstrating the value the Chickasaws continued to place on education. The Chickasaws could no longer control the type of education their children received, but that did not mean that they did not encourage it or value it. For the Chickasaws, literacy instruction had become a cultural tradition, and commencement, the symbol of that tradition, became a new kind of ceremony or ritual. In spite of the objectives of policymakers, literacy education was still an important method of tribal preservation for Chickasaws. Their children, educated at Bloomfield or Carter and later Chilocco, would one day reorganize the tribal government.

The Years After

After leaving Bloomfield or Carter, many women went on to attend Chilocco, an off-reservation Indian boarding school near Newkirk, Oklahoma. Ida Bell Hughes Martin, Juanita Keel Tate, Frances Griffin Robinson, Ora Lee Chuculate Woods, Pauline Williford Adkins, Fannye Williford Skaggs, Leona Williford Isaac, Claudine Williford King, Mary Pittman Parris, Clara Pittman Gatlin, and Ula Mae Pittman Welch all attended Chilocco for some length of time; many graduated. Some of the women with whom I spoke married immediately after leaving Bloomfield or Carter and started a family. Others finished high school and started families and started work, some for the Bureau of Indian Affairs. A few continued their education and received bachelor's and master's degrees. All of the women value the education they received and saw to it that their children were educated. Education had become tradition, and the legacy of Bloomfield and Carter is the belief instilled in the women that education is good — something to be sought, not just for themselves, but for their children. Graduates of Bloomfield and Carter wanted their children to attain higher levels of education than they had reached.

When I asked the women about their lives after Bloomfield and Carter, it was interesting to see what they included and what details they spent the most time discussing, since whatever they included was obviously what they considered to be the most important parts of their lives. The stories of Ora Lee Chuculate Woods (1930–36) and Claudine Williford King (1939–48) centered on education. Ora Lee sought higher education for herself; Claudine sought it for her children. Ora Lee expressed that she thought that education was the best thing a person could have. Every time she and her husband lived near a college, they found a way to attend and eventually earned graduate degrees. They live in Durant, the seat of the Choctaw Nation, a few blocks from Southeastern Oklahoma State University. In the following story, Ora Lee remembers how hard she and her husband, both Chilocco graduates, worked to put themselves through college:

> I could see that I could get a government loan, and they would let me work for my room and board, and they would send me to Southeastern on this government loan. . . . I came directly to Durant and went to OPC [Oklahoma Presbyterian College] and enrolled at Southeastern. And I stayed at Southeastern and went summer and winter right straight through, and I graduated in 1943. And while I was at Chilocco, I met my husband . . . he was a

year ahead of me, so he stayed at Chilocco doing post-graduate
work until I got out. . . . He's Chickasaw. And so he moved into
his folks' house and came to Southeastern, and I could live at OPC
and go to Southeastern. And that was in 1939, so in 1939 we enrolled in college, and in 1940 they mobilized the National Guard.
John joined the National Guard at Chilocco . . . so we were going
to get married when we finished college, but see our college was
interrupted . . . and he said . . . let's just go ahead and get married
when the semester ends . . . so we got married . . . when the draft
board called him . . . he said, "Well, I've got to go," and his boss
said . . . "We can get you out of that draft as easy as anything."
And he said, "No, I want to go. I'm trained, and it's my country,
and I want to defend it." He did his basic training, and I finished
with my class in 1943. . . . He felt the call to preach . . . and we
decided to . . . go to Shawnee so that he could go to OBU [Okla-
homa Baptist University]. . . . [He pastored] a church near Lufkin,
Texas . . . that was not far from . . . Stephen F. Austin College.
And he said, "This is just too close not to go to that school." So
he went to school there and got his master's in English . . .
and [Hardin-Simmons College asked] him to come and teach
English . . . so I went to Hardin-Simmons and got a master's in
history at the same college where he was teaching English.[105]

Claudine Williford King (1939–48) and her husband live in northern
Oklahoma, very near Chilocco, where they both worked at some point
in their lives. Claudine, although very proud of her own education and
accomplishments, was more interested in discussing the accomplishments of her five children. The following story demonstrates the value
Claudine places on education:

I went to high school there [Chilocco] and met my husband
there. . . . I graduated as valedictorian of the class of 1952. There
were 92 Indians in that class. . . . I chose to go to Hill's Business
University in Oklahoma City . . . we got married the fall after we

graduated from high school. . . . My husband had been a year ahead of me there. He is Creek. And he had been a year ahead of me, but when he had to go overseas with the 45th during the Korean War, so when he came back he was in my class . . . and we got married in the fall of 1952. . . . He went on to OSU [Oklahoma State University]. We stayed at Chilocco four years and lived there on the campus. . . . And then in 1956 we moved to Stillwater so that he could go to college . . . he went back to Chilocco in 1963 . . . and we have been here for over 30 years. . . . He worked for Chilocco for 22 years, and I worked here in town at an abstract company primarily because we have five children and they were in school here. . . . I did go to work at Chilocco as the registrar and worked there for seven years before it closed. And then both of us . . . were employed at an oil company and got good jobs . . . we had to put five kids through college . . . four of them [graduated] . . . the oldest is a computer electrical engineer. He is working on his Ph.D. right now . . . the second one is . . . the senior vice-president of operations for an oil company in Houston. . . . The third boy . . . is getting his master's in environmental engineering in December . . . our only daughter . . . got her master's in zoology . . . the youngest one lives and works in Kaw City . . . they are all self-sufficient.[106]

The years women spent in school first at Bloomfield or Carter and then at Chilocco were important because they shaped the women's values and beliefs. Many women call their classmates at Bloomfield, Carter, and Chilocco their family; they share the same stories. The schools designed to strip them of their identities as Indians actually reinforced that identity. Many women spent twelve years of their lives surrounded by nobody but other Indians. As a result, many women value their family — their Bloomfield and Carter Indian family — as much as the education they received.

Several women, graduates of Bloomfield or Carter and Chilocco, devoted much of their lives to Indian education and other Indian affairs.

Dorothy Wall Holt (1940–47) lives in Ardmore and worked at Carter Seminary for several years. In the following account, she describes her life after attending Carter:

> I was going to go to . . . Chilocco and then I met this guy . . . my future husband. . . . It was during the war, and all the men were gone . . . we thought that we wanted to get married, and so I got married real young, and my uncles had a fit when they came in from service, you know . . . then I went on and had my first baby at seventeen and then two more children, and I was real young with them growing up . . . and I did not work when they were young, but when they got up in high school, I went back to school and got my GED, and then I started working here at Carter for the Bureau of Indian Affairs. . . . I don't work for the tribe [now]. I work for Delta Community Action out of Duncan, and [Carter] just donates me office space here because I have volunteers here. I am supervisor of the foster grandparent program. . . . They help with the little kids and the young ones that come in.[107]

Although Dorothy is no longer employed by the Bureau of Indian Affairs (BIA), her office is located at Carter Seminary, and she currently serves as the president of the Bloomfield/Carter Alumni Association.

Like Dorothy, Frances Griffin Robinson (1927–29) also married young and spent much her life as a homemaker before working for the BIA. Her daughter Chiquita was named after the daughter of one of her favorite teachers at Bloomfield. Frances loved to work with children and began her career later in life by working for the BIA in several capacities, once at Carter Seminary. She commented: "I went one year [to Madill High School] . . . and then we went to Murray [in Tishomingo]. They had four years in high school and two in college there. . . . I didn't [finish]. I went ahead and married. . . . We were married twenty-seven years. Ended in divorce, and I went right to work for the BIA. No problems. Being up there and having a little bit of responsibility with children helped me get my job [at Carter]. . . . I was over the dormitories and guidance. Boy, I enjoyed my work with the kids."[108] Frances has always been active in the Bloomfield/Carter Alumni Association and has been a member of Ohoyohoma, a local club for American Indian women.

Juanita Keel Tate (1918), a product of Indian schools, was never involved in Indian education. Instead, Juanita, always involved in tribal affairs, is a well-respected family and tribal historian. Juanita's husband was not Chickasaw but always encouraged her participation in the tribe. In the following story, Juanita describes her life right after graduation and the early years of her marriage:

> I graduated from Chilocco in May 1928. . . . I was going to Ardmore Business College and he [my future husband] happened to be the manager of that . . . and I met Ernest. . . . I did some court reporting, and then I even opened a public stenographer's office there on main street. . . . I was trying to raise my brood of little children and do that too, and it just didn't work. So, I just closed that down, and then when Ernie studied law and opened his law office, well, I worked for him. . . . Ernest was a white man. He wasn't Chickasaw. . . . He wasn't Indian at all, and if anyone asked him to participate . . . he would always say — and I was glad he did — he would always say, "No, let the Indians do their own thing." So, if he could help in any way, of course, he did, to whatever extent was necessary.[109]

Juanita instilled her love of the tribe in her children and grandchildren. Her children are involved in tribal affairs and preservation activities, and her son, Charles Tate, has served as a tribal judge. One of her grandsons, Jerod Tate, has participated in the Americans for Indian Opportunity Ambassadors Program, a national leadership program founded by LaDonna Harris. A musician, he composed the score for a ballet, choreographed by his mother, based on the Trail of Tears.

Many of the women with whom I spoke loved their school years. Others were happy to leave and move on. All of the women, however, said that their studies at Bloomfield or Carter helped prepare them for whatever lay ahead in their futures. As many women remarked, the school "taught us everything we needed to get by."

Literacy for Home Living

Under federal control, administrators changed the organization, student population, and curriculum in ways that would help them achieve their purpose — the making of "all-around efficient citizens" who would be prepared to handle whatever life threw them. Students enrolled as students at Bloomfield and Carter as early as six years of age. As a result, the school, in effect, had to raise the students; consequently, the curriculum was designed to provide the students with different literacies–religious, social, academic, and domestic literacies– that would enable students to make some sort of lives for themselves and their families, the best lives they could.

Domestic literacy, what Pauline referred to as "home living," was the most heavily emphasized because at that time good women citizens were expected, no matter what else they did, to make good homes. The students at Bloomfield and Carter, frequently from rural and poor backgrounds, were expected to go back home in the summers and use their knowledge to help their families and then to begin their own families, families they would raise and educate. Attending Bloomfield or Carter was the first step in a continuing cycle of self-betterment and education.

Government officials, who saw literacy education as an efficient way to turn Indians into good citizens, took every possible step to acculturate the students. What they did not realize, however, was that segregating the students only made them closer. For the Chickasaws, literacy instruction was a tradition; they were used to the acculturation process. Policymakers and educators thought that acculturation meant that students would give up whatever characteristics made them Indian. Chickasaws knew that changing through acculturation did not have to mean giving up "Indianness" for "whiteness." Only tribes can decide what it means to be Indian. For the Chickasaw Nation, literacy education had always been a means of self-preservation, no matter who was in charge.

The Chickasaw Nation is proud of the education students received at Bloomfield and Carter under every administration in the school's history. Chickasaws have always considered the academy a good thing, no matter what the purpose of the school was at any given time, or whether or not they agreed with that purpose. That is the nature of literacy — no matter what the literacy teachers intend, literacy is finally used to achieve the goals of the learners.

I asked the women what they thought about the school, now, after years of reflection — what was the mission of the academy, what sort of life were they being prepared to lead? Their responses were at the same time very different, yet very much alike. Not surprisingly, several women gave more than one answer, demonstrating the complexity of their experiences and perhaps some ambivalence. They recognized that the school had many purposes, and it is understandable that the school meant so many different things to them. Some women think of Bloomfield as a place that showed them a different world and a different way to be in the world — they saw it as a place of opportunity. For example, Ora Lee Chuculate Woods (1930–36) believed that "[Eleanor Allen] had this attitude. . . . I tell you she really stirred a conscientiousness and awareness in the girls to be something bigger than that little school. . . . I really feel that she had the idea that she was training the girls to be leaders of the community." [110] Hettie McCauley King (1925–30) felt much the same way. She said emphatically that "[Bloomfield was preparing me] for a good life. Really to me it was inspiring. We were all proud to be there. I couldn't say anything against Bloomfield." [111]

A few women focused on the "preparatory" nature of the school, seeing it, not as a place where you were taken care of, but a place where you learned to take care of yourself. As Dorothy Wall Holt pointed out, "[Carter was preparing me] to be independent, and I am independent . . . we had to follow the rules, and if you learned that basically when you first came, that sticks with you all through your life. I mean you can be an individual and still . . . I try to make my way." [112] Like Dorothy, Claudine Williford King (1939–48) focused on preparation and independence. According to Claudine,

[They were preparing you to be] anything that you wanted to be. They emphasized that you could do whatever you thought you could do. They certainly equipped us academically for whatever. . . . I mean, it was mostly accepted that you would do that, go to school some place. Yes, they did encourage you to go to school, but they also taught you how to . . . all of the necessary things that you need to know if you weren't going to go to school . . . to cook and to sew and make a good home, you know. They were just trying to teach you everything they could, and they gave you a smattering of everything. [113]

Dorothy, Claudine, Ora, and Hettie answered the question in terms of what kind of life they believed Bloomfield or Carter was trying to prepare them for them as an individual. A few women, on the other hand, chose to discuss what the school was to trying to prepare them for collectively as Indian women. For example, Jeanne Liddell Cochran (1929–1933) contended that "the primary thing was to bring these Indian girls into the mainstream. I really think that was what they were striving for, which a lot of people think is cruel. But it is like my grandmother said, . . . the way of the Indian is gone, and you need to learn the way of the white people because they are in charge . . . so we knew that when we went by the fact that she would not let us learn the Chickasaw language. We knew it. And I think that was the purpose of it." [114]

Dorothy valued the school for teaching her to be an independent individual but, like Jeanne, realized the school had another purpose. She said that the objective was "to make white people out of Indians . . . really I think . . . bottom line . . . We just kind of went along with it." She tried to explain her family's reasoning for "going along with it." She said, "I look back and I think it is because my grandfather was a white man, my dad was a white man, and my grandmother and my mother probably thought. . . . especially my grandmother probably thought that was the best for us." She has tried to make up for this as an adult in a number of ways. According to Dorothy, "after I got grown, I wanted to know all about my history. So I have to get out and look that up." [115]

Pauline Williford Adkins's (1932–41) answer to my question about the mission of Bloomfield or Carter was very similar to Dorothy's and Jeanne's, yet her answer points out how attitudes have changed over the years. Pauline remarked, "It seems like going back to your own tribe or anything like that came later on in years. After I got out of school, they wanted everybody to go back to their own way of living and . . . well, their language and everything like that. I believe that came after I got out of school . . . they were trying to prepare us for the white man's world . . . to get out and mingle with other people besides our own . . . besides Indians." [116]

Nevertheless, no matter how any of the women felt about the school's desire to "change" them, most, if not all, firmly stated that they appreciated all of the education they got. Jeanne Liddell Cochran (1929–33), for example, felt that Bloomfield was an excellent school and stated that she would not trade her days there for anything. She remarked:

> You will hear the girls refer to that as a finishing school because we were taught academics, we were taught the arts. We had our classes. We had to learn art, you know the paintings and such as that. We had to know that. We had music. We . . . had to learn our proper manners. And that is what they were trying to do, and the way they taught is like a very expensive finishing school today . . . and when they did away with it, I thought how terrible. . . . You could not have asked for a better school anywhere in the United States than that was. [117]

Juanita Keel Tate (1918) and Frances Griffin Robinson (1927–29) expressed that the school enabled them to succeed as adults in the larger community. Juanita said the Bloomfield "prepared [us] for life . . . to be good citizens."[118] Frances agreed, saying that "[Because of] what I learned . . . I knew how to carry on in a job."[119] Both Juanita and Frances have spent much of their lives working in Indian communities.

Interestingly, Fannye Williford Skaggs and Leona Williford Isaac (1933–47) agree that Carter prepared students to go out in the world, but they focused more in their answer on the ways in which it prepared students to go back home. They responded, "They were preparing us to go back. The ability to be able to learn . . . I had to learn to milk a goat, and . . . I don't think the expectations were that they would . . . it wouldn't make any difference what they were doing, [students] would still go back to the wood stove and the cow and that type of living anyway. So I think it was just accepted."[120]

What was the school's mission? According to the women with whom I talked, it taught students to go back home, to go out into the world, to be independent, to be ladies, and to be aware of their possibilities. Did the school "change" them? I do not believe that the school transformed students from Indians into whites. Identity is much more complicated than that, and the women I interviewed, all of mixed heritage, seem to recognize the complexity of their identities, or perhaps they see having a mixed identity as very simple indeed. At any rate, they seem to accept their identities as a matter of fact, not as a matter of crisis. I do believe that the school definitely changed the students and impacted their lives in powerful ways. The following response of Claudine Williford King (1939–48) somehow sums up the variety of perspectives the women presented:

[The mission at Carter] was to educate the Indian children that came there so that they could fit into the mainstream and make a good life for themselves. I don't . . . you know, I have heard comments that they were trying to take away their Indian heritage. I don't think that's right. . . . What they were trying to do was . . . or I felt like, and did a very good job of it, was to equip us to get by in the world the way it was and is. They did not put down the Indians. They didn't want us to talk Indian . . . and I regret that. . . . I wish they had not done that. But it was one way that they . . . We learned the English language thoroughly and completely and how to write and how to express ourselves and get along.[121]

Perhaps Clara, Mary, and Ula Mae said it the best: "That's what they were doing . . . teaching us how to live."[122]

5
Nananumpoli otalhli (To End the Story)

※

We at Carter Seminary believe that a free society is dependent upon education for the transmission of values, traditions, and ideals. We believe that education must enhance the dignity of the individual. Dignity connotes knowledge, self-confidence, self-discipline, and responsibility. — CARTER SEMINARY PHILOS-OPHY, *present day*

Taped on the wall above my desk are two pieces of paper. One is a copy of a page from the guest register of the Bloomfield/Carter reunion, dated May 20, 1978. My grandmother's name is on it. Her handwriting looks like my father's. The other piece of paper is a list of reminders I typed up myself—things I wanted to think about as I wrote. The first item on the list says, "Tell the story"; the second, "Be true to the story." I look again at the list of signatures on the guest book page and see names I recognize. Frances Griffin Robinson signed right under my grandmother, which is not surprising; they probably went together. Dorothy Wall Holt was there that day, too. I do not recognize the other names. Although those signatures belong to women I have never met, I do know that this story is their story, too. When I wrote "Be true to the story," I was also, in a sense, writing, "Be true to the women." Literacy is interesting: although it is something one individual teaches another, its legacy affects many. The current Carter Seminary philosophy states that education is used "for the transmission of values, traditions, and ideals." Education not only transmits values, traditions, and ideals; education, literacy, is a value, a tradition, and is always tied to an ideal—we believe in education because of what we hope it will bring us. Consequently, seeking education is one of the most positive, hopeful actions an individual can perform. I look at the signatures on the guest book, knowing that these women, Bloomfield and Carter alums, left their legacy: a hope for the future and a belief that education is good and valuable.

Acculturation, Preservation, and Identity

Literacy is a question of value and a question of purpose. Missionaries valued religious literacy for conversion, Chickasaws valued social literacy for competitive success and survival, and federal government officials valued domestic literacy for home living. The underlying, but conscious, purpose of the school under every administration was acculturation. The major tension at the heart of this study, of this school, is the tension between what seem to be two opposing poles: assimilation and preservation.

Under mission and Chickasaw control, the Chickasaws were fighting for their survival. Their very continuance as a nation was dependent on their ability to negotiate in a white world. Their ability and willingness to acculturate became their strength. Education became their weapon. Many people would see this acculturation as dying as a culture, not as surviving. But what were their choices? To change and continue on, or to resist and dissolve? Cultures are dynamic, active, and ever changing. A static culture is not a living one. Society allows other cultures to change, so why not Indians? Why not the Chickasaws? The Chickasaws chose to change, and in changing they maintained their identity, they preserved their identity. Their choice did not make them any less Chickasaw. As Devon Mihesuah states, "While it is tempting to define 'Indianness' by non-Indian standards—and that is indeed the norm—to do so is inappropriate. Tribes decide their identity for themselves." [1]

The school did strip the students of their traditions and heritage. Under federal control, students were not taught Indian history. They were not allowed to speak their Native languages and were even punished for it. Planned cultural activities probably did not take place often, if ever. A few women mentioned dressing up like Indians for a play or recording Indian chants at the local radio station. These activities could be classified as "cultural"; however, they are not the activities that really count. Many women left home at the age of six to spend the next several years, perhaps as many as twelve, at Bloomfield or Carter and then Chilocco—surrounded by other Indians. The purpose of the boarding academies may have been assimilation, but the students were, in fact, segregated. Ironically, the government got the students ready for the mainstream by making sure that they associated with no one but other Indians for the whole of their formative years. Many women speak of their classmates at Bloomfield or Carter and later at Chilocco as family. In the following story, Claudine Williford King, a student at Carter in the 1940s, demonstrates just how close—just how much like family—boarding school students can become.

> It was just a wonderful place to be, and I made lifelong friends there. And I feel very much a part of the Indian world. My husband and I both. He was in a grade school for boys . . . Indian grade school. . . . We went to a powwow this spring. . . . But we felt at home. It was a good feeling to hear the drums and listen and visit with old friends, you know. That's the way we grew up. And a lot of that was the same feeling you have when you get together with Carter Seminary girls. They are more like sisters than anything else because you lived with them for eight years . . . a lot of people go to [reunions] and it's a special feeling at those boarding schools when you lived with someone for eight years. They become as much family to you as your own family . . . and another story . . . there was a tornado that went near here a couple of years ago. And somehow it got picked up on the national news—and now understand that we have five children and a state full of relatives here—but the phone rang, and it was one of our Chilocco classmates from Los Angeles who said, "Are you guys all right? We saw on the television that you had a tornado there." Well, that's just the kind

of family feeling you had at Carter and also at Chilocco. Made very
close bonds. When my husband was in the military, and they were
called up to active duty, they were down in Louisiana, and they
were playing softball outside the barracks and talking and laughing, and he said at the next barracks there was a kid sitting on the
step crying. And one of the captains came over there . . . my husband was a sergeant, and he said to him . . . "What are you guys
doing over here? How is it that all of your guys . . . they don't seem
to be having the problems ours are? They are homesick. They don't
know one another. They don't know what to do with themselves."
He said, "You guys are just all out here just talking and laughing
and having a good time." And he [my husband] said, "Well, that's
because we're already like a family unit. We have lived together for
years." And so it was an advantage to them. And I think one reason
there were so many Medal of Honor winners from that all-Indian
company from Chilocco is because they were with their family and
fighting for guys that they had known and lived with all their lives.[2]

Claudine and her classmates at Carter and Chilocco became family
because of the stories they share. Many women met their husbands at
Chilocco and married after high school. Of the women with whom I
spoke, most attend Bloomfield/Carter and Chilocco reunions. Many are
active in or keep up with tribal affairs. Some have made an effort to
learn their history after their school years. Many attend tribal events,
and some have been members of Ohoyohoma, a local club for Native
American women. Two of the women later worked for the Bureau of
Indian Affairs at Carter. One woman is a family and tribal historian. Few
women left their families and communities after school; most started
their own families in or near their hometowns and are still there today.
The school did serve as a tool of assimilation, but it also served, at the
same time, to preserve—to instill in them a common bond and identity
as Indians. However, their identities as Indians do not make them feel
less American. In fact, most are patriotic citizens and proud of their
country. For most of these women, having citizenship in two nations

does not cause a conflict of identity; the two are very intertwined and mixed—-they are *Americans* and *Indians*, they are *American Indians*.

At last I am forced to ask myself what I think about the literacy curricula offered at Bloomfield and Carter, its purposes, its results. This story began with my grandma and comes back full circle to her. For my grandma and our family, that she was a Bloomfield student is a matter of some pride, a privilege, the beginning of an important chain, for Grandma saw to it that my father finished high school and had the chance to attend college. My own parents encouraged me to attend graduate school and to teach. And our educations have not served to alienate us from our tribe but have encouraged our continuing participation. So for me, all in all, the good with the bad, the literacy education at Bloomfield and Carter did cause a loss of culture, which was painful for many. But change is painful, and with change is *continuance*, something I value.

Reflection

I asked each woman what she now thought of her education at Bloomfield or Carter, after all these years of reflection. Not surprisingly, many women gave more than one response. Their answers were varied and seemed to depend on what aspects of the school helped them most later in life. Frances and Jeanne focused on the quality of the education itself, with which they were very pleased. For example, Frances Griffin Robinson (1927–29), comparing her experience at Bloomfield to her experience at public school, remarked, "I made straight A's at [public school]. But we [at Bloomfield] were way ahead of the other students at other schools . . . at that time, it was so demanding. You know, you just didn't get by with anything but doing your best. . . . I really do [think it was superior]." [3] Jeanne Liddell Cochran (1929–33) had to transfer to a public school after the fourth grade, much to her dismay. As she said, "I loved it, I loved it. I was never so upset in my life as when I had to leave there." She was particularly impressed with the academic standards the school maintained, something of which she was not aware until her transfer to public schools. She commented, "I can look back now and realize it was more advanced than public school, because when I left at the end of the fourth grade, they put me either in the sixth or seventh grade." [4]

A few other women's comments highlighted the fact that it was a "privilege" to go a "finishing school" like Bloomfield. Hettie McCauley King (1925–30), for example, remarked, "Oh, I think it was really great. I had such a good time when I was there. The teachers were really good . . . top notch. . . . One of the teachers told me that it was like a finishing school." [5] Dorothy Wall Holt (1940–47) remembered feeling well cared for and special. According to Dorothy, "I felt like it was so neat when we went to school. We felt privileged. . . . I felt special because I was treated real well." [6] Pauline Williford Adkins (1932–41) commented on how much learning "manners and etiquette" helped her later in life: "[It helped me with] manners and how to present yourself and meet the public and everything like that. . . . And I worked out in the public for [years]." [7]

Ora Lee Chuculate Woods not only discussed the finishing school atmosphere of the school but went on to say that the school inspired her to be "something more." According to Ora Lee, "We wanted to be the best, and we wanted to be ladies, and we wanted to excel at everything we did. We had to have the nicest and cleanest building, and we wanted to pass every examination and wanted to do everything we could to beat the Wheelock [Choctaw] school. . . . [I enjoyed my education] very much." [8]

Fannye Williford Skaggs and Leona Williford Isaac (1933–47) agreed that the academic standards of the school were good and felt that the social skills they learned stood them in good stead. Leona, however, realized as an adult how "isolated" they were at school and had mixed feelings about that fact. According to Leona,

I think the education part . . . was all right. It was the segregation that we had that was the [biggest disadvantage] . . . I wasn't aware [at that time]. . . . Because we didn't ever get mixed with anyone. . . . You went back home and . . . you knew those people from the time they were in the cradle, you know, or they knew you. . . . I feel like that as far as the benefit part, I feel like we did learn, because they didn't pass you unless you learned. And a lot of the other schools, they just passed you along. Or they do now. Yeah, you either learned it or you didn't go to the next grade. . . . But to become aware of that [segregation] . . . I had to leave to know how segregated it was. It was just one little isolated spot. You had no access to radios, newspapers . . . no family came in to . . . no one told you news. . . . You know, it was like . . . it is like something that you are not aware of until after you have left it, or that was the way it was with me . . . you know, I thought we were hundreds of miles from home. I did. And I thought when some little girl ran off, and they brought her back in a government car—which happened—I thought how brave she was.[9]

Leona's comment that she thought she was "hundreds of miles from home" even though she was not reminds us again how much students had to rely on each other for support; nearly every woman I interviewed referred to her classmates as family.

Pauline, Mary, Clara, and Ula Mae talked more about the practical subjects taught at Bloomfield and Carter. For example, Pauline Williford Adkins (1932–41) observed that "the kids are going to school in Ardmore now, and they are probably getting more book learning than we really got—but they are not getting the . . . well, the home living or whatever you would call it . . . the difference there." According to Pauline, the practical, home economic subjects have been just as much or more useful than academic subjects. She commented, "Well, I just appreciate what I did learn by going to school out there. It is just altogether different from what it is now. . . . I think it was worthwhile."[10] Like Pauline, Mary Pittman Parris, Clara Pittman Gatlin, and Ula Mae Pittman Welch (1935–47) felt they benefited as adults from the home economic subjects, the "detail" assignments, and the overall discipline taught at the school. They stated: "I really do [think we had a good education there]. They taught us manners, to be neat and clean, and you know . . . like now you know if you have to get up at a certain time . . . if you do just have a job, just a plain job, you knew to get up and get there on time. Not be late, you know, and . . . everything. I really . . . I think that it really helped us." [11]

Claudine Williford King (1939–48) discussed both academic and practical subjects in her response. However, she believes that what she really got from her experience at Carter were larger life lessons like discipline and self-motivation. Of further significance, she tied her own educational experiences and successes directly to her children's, reminding us of the legacy of literacy. Claudine's remarks are reflective of feelings most women expressed, and the following passage serves as a sort of summary of them all: "We had good teachers. They taught us a lot of useful things. Taught us discipline. I mean, self-motivation and discipline, which you need to succeed. And I think a lot of young people these days lack that. They taught us that we could do anything that we wanted to do. There are a lot of kids who went through Carter Seminary and Chilocco who have done very well and whose children have done very well. So it was a good thing." [12]

Endings

New Mexico, 1999. Carter Seminary closed its doors as a boarding school for girls in 1949. Fifty years later and seven hundred miles away, I find myself writing a conclusion to this book, but not an ending to the story. I would like to write this conclusion at home, in Oklahoma, but it is fall, the season for starting school, and I am teaching school, teaching *English* of all things, and cannot leave right now. But perhaps there is something appropriate about that after all. I look again at the list of signatures. The signatures symbolize so much; each one is a record of a person, an identity in a particular place and time; each one is an act, perhaps the most basic act, of individual literacy. Each name signifies a story, and together, the names give rise to the story of Bloomfield—the story I am telling now.

I read my grandmother's name, *Ida Pratt Cobb*. She died when I was seven; in July of 1996, I asked Hettie McCauley King what she was like—I said I wished I had known her better. Hettie said to me, "Well, you missed a lot, because she was a fine person. And a lot of fun." It is 1999, and since that summer day three years ago, I have read and imagined and listened and told, and now I can say this: Yes, Hettie, yes, she was.

The legacy my grandma left me is the same legacy all of the women who attended Bloomfield and Carter left their children and grandchildren and great-grandchildren—a legacy of hope and hardiness, of family and friendship, a belief in tradition, but an ability to change. I have been looking for the right words *nananumpoli otalhli*, to end the story, but I do not have them, cannot have them, because I know that listening to stories and telling them is a matter of continuance. And in that spirit, I will not end this story—I will add my name.

Amanda J. Cobb
November 1, 1999

Biographies

PAULINE WILLIFORD ADKINS (Chickasaw)

Pauline Williford Adkins was born near Lebanon, Oklahoma, in January 1926. She attended Bloomfield and Carter from 1932 to 1941 and Chilocco from 1941 to 1943. After leaving Chilocco, Pauline attended Oak Cliff Business School in Dallas and worked in Dallas for the Dr. Pepper Company for many years. Pauline attends the Bloomfield/Carter and Chilocco reunions and served as secretary/treasurer of the Bloomfield/Carter Alumni Association for ten years. She has served as secretary of the Southeast Chapter of the Chilocco Indian School Alumni Association as well and is currently a member of the Chickasaw Alliance. Pauline has one son and two grandchildren. She is the double first cousin of Fannye Williford Skaggs, Leona Williford Isaac, and Ida Mae Pratt Cobb, a first cousin of Frances Griffin Robinson, and a cousin of Juanita Keel Tate. Pauline currently lives in the same place she was born, approximately two miles north of Lebanon, Oklahoma.

FANNY HUGHES BASS (Chickasaw)

Born in Connorville, Oklahoma, in 1898, Fanny Hughes Bass attended Bloomfield between 1911 and 1914. Her mother, Mamie Alexander Hughes, attended the Burney Institute, also known as the Lebanon Orphan's Institute. After her schooling, Fanny married Grady Bass. Fanny was the sister of Ida Bell Hughes Martin and Van Noy Hughes. Fanny was well known for her interest and work in arts and crafts, particularly for her crochet work. She spent most of her life in Tishomingo, Oklahoma, the original seat of the Chickasaw Nation, and died at the age of 100 in 1998.

JEANNE LIDDELL COCHRAN (Chickasaw)
Jeanne Liddell Cochran was born in Love County, Oklahoma, just south of Marietta in March 1923. She attended Bloomfield/Carter from 1929 to 1933. Her mother, Minnie Keel Liddell, attended Old Bloomfield and the Burney Institute. Jeanne worked for twenty-one years for Brown Oil and Tool Incorporated in Houston, Texas. She has two children, John Eugene Ellis and Beverly Maree Ellis, and is married to Chudleigh B. Cochran. Jeanne enjoys ballroom dancing and sewing and has served as the president of the Alpha Omega Reading Club in Houston, where she currently resides. She is a cousin of Juanita Keel Tate. Jeanne still owns her mother's house south of Marietta and returns there frequently.

CLARA PITTMAN GATLIN (Choctaw)
Clara Pittman Gatlin was born in Bennington, Oklahoma, in July 1934. She attended Carter Seminary from 1940 to 1947 and continued her education at Chilocco, from which she graduated in 1953. Clara has three children, eight grandchildren, and two great-grandchildren, with whom she loves to spend time. Clara enjoys gardening and reading and is active as a Jehovah's Witness. She made many good friends at Carter and appreciates attending the school. Clara's mother was a full-blood Mississippi Choctaw and raised nine children. Clara's sisters, Mary Pittman Parris, Ula Mae Pittman Welch, and Josie Pittman Gage, also attended Carter Seminary and Chilocco. Her brothers attended the Jones Academy, a coeducational boarding school run by the Choctaw Nation. Clara currently lives in Silo, Oklahoma, just west of Durant.

DOROTHY WALL HOLT (Choctaw)
Dorothy Wall Holt was born April 5, 1931, in Maysville, Oklahoma, and raised in Ardmore. She attended Carter Seminary from 1940 to 1947.

Dorothy is active in the Bloomfield/Carter Alumni Association and currently serves as president. Her aunt, Josephine Sewell Cantrell, attended Haskell. Dorothy's grandmother, Nettie Jack, a full-blood Mississippi Choctaw, came to Indian Territory on the second removal. Her father, John Baptist Wall, is deceased, and her mother, Mary Wall, resides in Ardmore. Dorothy had three children, Jimmy Don Grayham, Gary Grayham, and Pattie Dawn Grayham. Jimmy Don, a retired major in the U.S. Armed Forces, passed away in March 1999. Dorothy has seven grandchildren: Christy, Justin, Jason, Rhoda, Tre', Samantha, and Dawnthia. She currently lives in Ardmore and works at Carter Seminary for Delta Community Action.

LEONA WILLIFORD ISAAC (Chickasaw)
Born in 1927 in Lebanon, Oklahoma, Leona Williford Isaac attended Bloomfield/Carter from 1933 to 1941 and graduated from Chilocco in 1946. Leona worked for many years for the Oklahoma City Public School System. She has four children, ten grandchildren, and two greatgrandchildren. Leona, a resident of Moore, Oklahoma, said that her primary hobbies are gardening, walking, and reading, which she grew to love while at Carter. She remarked, "I don't know what I'd do without my glasses or my books." Leona is the sister of Fannye Williford Skaggs. She is also the double first cousin of Pauline Williford Adkins and Ida Mae Pratt Cobb, a first cousin of Frances Griffin Robinson, an aunt of Claudine Williford King, and a cousin of Juanita Keel Tate.

CLAUDINE WILLIFORD KING (Chickasaw)
Claudine Williford King was born in Marshall County, Oklahoma, just north of Lebanon. She attended Carter Seminary from 1939 to 1948 and then Chilocco, from which she graduated as valedictorian. She met her husband, John, a member of the Creek Nation, at Chilocco. They have five children. Claudine and her husband both worked for many years at Chilocco. After the school closed, they worked for an oil company until their retirement. They currently live in northern Oklahoma, near Chi-

locco, and frequently attend Chilocco reunions. Claudine is the niece of Fannye Williford Skaggs and Leona Williford Isaac and a cousin of Juanita Keel Tate.

HETTIE MCCAULEY KING (Chickasaw)
Hettie McCauley King was born in Ardmore, Oklahoma, and attended Bloomfield Academy between 1925 and 1930. Hettie has attended Bloomfield/Carter reunions and was a member of Ohoyohoma, an organization for American Indian women. Her mother, Kizzie Kernel McCauley, was a graduate of Old Bloomfield. Hettie married Raymond King, who worked at Tinker Air Force Base following his service in the U.S. Army Third Armored Division. They have two foster grandchildren, Mark and Mia Methvin. Hettie lived much of her life in Ardmore, but currently resides in Edmond, Oklahoma, where she is a member of the Church of Christ. She is currently working on her autobiography.

IDA BELL HUGHES MARTIN (Chickasaw)
Ida Bell Hughes Martin, the sister of Fanny Hughes Bass and Van Noy Hughes, was born in Connorville, Oklahoma, and attended Bloomfield in the 1920s. After leaving Bloomfield, Ida attended Riverside, a federally run boarding school in New Mexico, where she learned to weave on a loom. Ida's mother, Mamie Alexander Hughes, attended Burney Institute in Lebanon, Oklahoma. Ida has two children, Sherry Sue Horton and Robert Martin. She currently resides in Tishomingo, Oklahoma.

MARY PITTMAN PARRIS (Choctaw)
Mary Pittman Parris was born in Bennington, Oklahoma, which is near Durant, the seat of the Choctaw Nation. She attended Carter Seminary from approximately 1935 to 1942 and continued her education at Chilocco. Mary attends Bloomfield/Carter reunions. One of nine children, she is the sister of Ula Mae Pittman Welch, Clara Pittman Gatlin, and Josie Pittman Gage. She currently lives in Durant and is a Jehovah's Witness.

FRANCES GRIFFIN ROBINSON (Chickasaw)

Frances Griffin Robinson was born in Lebanon, Oklahoma, and attended Bloomfield from 1927 to 1929. After leaving Bloomfield, Frances attended Murray State College in Tishomingo, which was then a high school and junior college. In addition to homemaking, Frances worked at several schools, including Carter Seminary, for the Bureau of Indian Affairs. She has one daughter, Chiquita, and two grandchildren, Jaquelyn and John Pat. Frances is a first cousin of Ida Mae Pratt Cobb, Pauline Williford Adkins, Leona Williford Isaac, and Fannye Williford Skaggs and a cousin of Claudine Williford King and Juanita Keel Tate. Frances lives in Lebanon, only a few miles from her birthplace. She is a member of the Chickasaw Alliance and enjoys going to the Chickasaw Community Center in Ardmore and Bloomfield/Carter reunions.

FANNYE WILLIFORD SKAGGS (Chickasaw)

Fannye Williford Skaggs was born in Lebanon, Oklahoma, in 1932 and is a sister of Leona Williford Isaac. She is also the double first cousin of Pauline Williford Adkins and Ida Mae Pratt Cobb, a first cousin of Frances Griffin Robinson, an aunt of Claudine Williford King, and a cousin of Juanita Keel Tate. Fannye attended Carter Seminary from 1939 to 1947. Her mother, Alice, attended the Burney Institute. Fannye went to high school at Chilocco and worked for the U.S. Department of Navy in Washington DC following her graduation in 1951. After moving back to Oklahoma, Fannye married and has two step-children and seven grandchildren. She worked for Red Ball Motor Freight in Oklahoma City for many years. She spends her free time gardening and reading and still lives in Oklahoma City.

JUANITA KEEL TATE (Chickasaw)

Juanita Keel Tate was born in Ardmore, Oklahoma, in 1910 and attended Bloomfield Seminary in 1918. Her mother, Lula Potts Keel, was a graduate of Old Bloomfield. Juanita graduated from Chilocco in 1928. She married Ernest W. Tate, an attorney, and became a legal secretary. Juanita has attended Bacone College in Muskogee, Oklahoma, Southeastern Oklahoma State University in Durant, Oklahoma, and East Central University in Ada, Oklahoma. She has three children, Charles Guy Tate, Roberta Ann Tate Boland, and Gwendolyn Tate Gentry, and several grandchildren and great-grandchildren. Juanita is a relative of Ida Mae Pratt Cobb, Frances Griffin Robinson, Pauline Williford Adkins, Fannye Williford Skaggs, Leona Williford Isaac, Claudine Williford King, Jeanne Liddell Cochran, Fannye Hughes Bass, and Ida Bell Hughes Martin. Juanita, who still lives in Ardmore, is active in tribal affairs and the Chickasaw Alliance. She is presently historian of the Chickasaw Chapter of the United Daughters of the Confederacy, a member of the National and Southeast Chapters of the Chilocco Indian School Alumni Association, and a member of the Greater Southwest Historical and Genealogical Society. She has been inducted into the Greater Southwest Historical Society Hall of Fame and the Chilocco Alumni Association Hall of Fame. She has served as president of both the Keel Cemetery Association and the Ohoyohoma Club. She is also a member of the Bloomfield/Carter Alumni Association and attends Bloomfield and Chilocco reunions. Juanita is much respected as a historian and genealogist.

ULA MAE PITTMAN WELCH (Choctaw)

Ula Mae Pittman Welch was born May 1, 1932, in Bennington, Oklahoma, which is near Durant, the seat of the Choctaw Nation. She is the sister of Mary Pittman Parris, Clara Pittman Gatlin, and Josie Pittman Gage. She attended Carter Seminary from 1940 to 1947 and went on to school at Chilocco, where she graduated in 1951. Her mother, a full-blood Mississippi Choctaw, raised nine children, all of whom attended boarding academies. Ula Mae married Ova J. Welch and has one son, Danny, and three grandsons, Charleton, Christopher, and Kyle, and three great-grandchildren, Brittany, Matthew Jay, and Darcy. All of her family lives in Durant. She is an active member of both the Bloomfield/Carter Alumni Association and the Chilocco Indian School Alumni Association. She enjoys reading, sewing, crocheting, and cooking. She loves to make treats for friends and social gatherings. She also likes to travel and has had the opportunity to travel to California, Florida, and New York as a Jehovah's Witness. She lives in Durant.

ORA LEE CHUCULATE WOODS (Cherokee)
Elmira Ora Lee Chuculate Woods was born in Sequoyah County, Oklahoma, in 1921 and attended Bloomfield/Carter from 1930 to 1936. She continued her education at Chilocco and after graduating attended Southeastern Oklahoma State University in Durant. She went on to earn two master's degrees, one in Education and one in History, from Hardin-Simmons University. Ora Lee married John Woods and raised five beautiful children, three of whom are living. She has six grandchildren. Ora Lee has served as president of the Bloomfield/Carter Alumni Association and has been an active member of the Baptist Church. She crochets and thoroughly enjoys making afghans. Ora Lee and her husband lived for many years in Durant but now reside in Owasso, Oklahoma.

In Memory of

IDA MAE PRATT COBB (Chickasaw)
Ida Mae Pratt Cobb, known most of her life as Dinah, was born in Indian Territory on July 3, 1907, the year of Oklahoma statehood. She lived her whole life just north of Lebanon, where she was born. She attended Bloomfield Academy from 1924 to 1926. Dinah, my grandmother, married Trueman Calvin Cobb, a farmer and rancher in 1929. They had two children, John G. Cobb of Ardmore, Oklahoma, and Murielene Cobb Potts, who lives in Lebanon on the family's farm. Dinah and Trueman had five grandchildren, Ed, George, and Steve Potts, Dinah Elizabeth Cobb McCraw, and Amanda Cobb. Dinah was the double first cousin of Pauline Williford Adkins, Fannye Williford Skaggs, and Leona Williford Isaac, a first cousin of Frances Griffin Robinson, and a cousin of Juanita Keel Tate. Dinah was, by all accounts, "a great favorite" of everyone who knew her. She died in 1978.

JOSIE PITTMAN GAGE

Clara Pittman Gatlin, Mary Pittman Parris, and Ula Mae Pittman Welch would like to dedicate their participation in this book in the loving memory of their sister, Josie Pittman Gage, who passed away in 1998. Josie attended Carter Seminary with her sisters, and all of the memories and stories they shared are also hers. They love their sister very much.

Notes

For Grandma

1 Ortiz, *Woven Stone*, 9.
2 Ortiz, *Woven Stone*, 10.
3 Kenny, *Tekonwatonti/Molly Brant*, 52–53.
4 Kenny, *Tekonwatonti/Molly Brant*, 193.
5 Momaday, *The Names*, 22.
6 Momaday, *The Names*, 26.

1. To Start to Tell a Story

1 Prucha, *American Indian Policy in Crisis*, 63–67.
2 Prucha, *American Indian Policy in Crisis*, 133.
3 Prucha, *American Indian Policy in Crisis*, 151–52.
4 Adams, *Education for Extinction*, 8, 20; Button and Provenzo, *History of Education and Culture in America*, 138; Prucha, *American Indian Policy in Crisis*, 103.
5 Prucha, *American Indian Policy in Crisis*, 193.
6 Prucha, *American Indian Policy in Crisis*, 84; James E. Rhoads, quoted in Lake Mohonk Conference proceedings, 1885, 6.
7 Rhoads, Lake Mohonk Conference proceedings, 1884, 8; Adams, *Education for Extinction*, 16–17.
8 Clinton B. Fisk, quoted in Lake Mohonk Conference proceedings, 1885, 4.
9 H. Jackson, *A Century of Dishonor*.
10 Adams, *Education for Extinction*, 11.
11 Prucha, *American Indian Policy in Crisis*, 403; Coleman, *American Indian Children at School*, 46.
12 Albert K. Smiley, quoted in Lake Mohonk Conference proceedings, 1885, 1.
13 Prucha, *American Indian Policy in Crisis*, 168.
14 Adams, *Education for Extinction*, 18.

15   Ellis, *To Change Them Forever*, 9.
16   Adams, *Education for Extinction*, 19; Prucha, *American Indian Policy in Crisis*, 156.
17   Merril E. Gates, quoted in Lake Mohonk Conference proceedings, 1891, 9.
18   Adams, *Education for Extinction*; Child, *Boarding School Seasons*; Coleman, *American Indian Children at School*; Ellis, *To Change Them Forever*; Lomawaima, *They Called It Prairie Light*; McBeth, *Ethnic Identity and the Boarding School Experience*; Szasz, *Education and the American Indian*.
19   Hobbs, *Nineteenth-Century Women Learn to Write*, 4.
20   Ellis, *To Change Them Forever*, 196.
21   Adams, *Education for Extinction*, x.
22   Berlin, *Rhetoric and Reality*, 1.
23   Knoblauch, "Literacy and the Politics of Education," 75–76.
24   Street, *Literacy in Theory and Practice*, 8.
25   Tchudi and Morris, *The New Literacy*, 12.
26   Street, *Literacy in Theory and Practice*, 109; Graff, *The Literacy Myth*, 289.
27   Prucha, *American Indian Policy in Crisis*, 271.
28   John H. Oberly, quoted in Lake Mohonk Conference proceedings, 1885, 61–62.
29   Street, *Social Literacies*, 3.

2.   Chickasaw Children Go to School
 1   Spring, *The American School*, 134.
 2   Gibson, *The Chickasaws*, 4; M. Wright, *Indian Tribes of Oklahoma*, 84.
 3   Cushman, *Choctaw, Chickasaw and Natchez Indians*, 362; Hudson, *The Southeastern Indians*, 23; M. Wright, *Indian Tribes of Oklahoma*, 84.
 4   Galloway, *Choctaw Genesis*, 331, 334; Cushman, *Choctaw, Chickasaw and Natchez Indians*, 358.
 5   Galloway, *Choctaw Genesis*, 335.
 6   Cushman, *Choctaw, Chickasaw and Natchez Indians*, 362.
 7   Gibson, *The Chickasaws*, 397.
 8   Cushman, *Choctaw, Chickasaw and Natchez Indians*, 397.
 9   Hudson, *The Southeastern Indians*, 115; Gibson, *The Chickasaws*, 32.
10   M. Wright, *Indian Tribes of Oklahoma*, 86.
11   Gibson, *The Chickasaws*, 6; M. Wright, *Indian Tribes of Oklahoma*, 86.
12   Hudson, *The Southeastern Indians*, 213–16.
13   M. Wright, *Indian Tribes of Oklahoma*, 86–87.
14   Gibson, *The Chickasaws*, 18.
15   Cushman, *Choctaw, Chickasaw and Natchez Indians*, 435.
16   Cushman, *Choctaw, Chickasaw and Natchez Indians*, 403; M. Wright, *Indian Tribes of Oklahoma*, 87.

17 Gibson, The Chickasaws, 12.

18 Gibson, The Chickasaws, 9–10.

19 Cushman, Choctaw, Chickasaw and Natchez Indians, 404; Gibson, The Chickasaws, 11; Galloway, Choctaw Genesis, 296; Hudson, The Southeastern Indians, 335.

20 Hudson, The Southeastern Indians, 365–75.

21 M. Wright, Indian Tribes of Oklahoma, 86.

22 Gibson, The Chickasaws, 4.

23 Cushman, Choctaw, Chickasaw and Natchez Indians, 414.

24 M. Wright, Indian Tribes of Oklahoma, 87.

25 M. Wright, Indian Tribes of Oklahoma, 88.

26 Gibson, The Chickasaws, 80–124.

27 Gibson, The Chickasaws, 107–8.

28 Prucha, Documents in United States Indian Policy, 33; Cremin, American Education: The National Experience, 234; Spring, The American School, 133.

29 Button and Provenzo, History of Education and Culture in America, 135.

30 Gibson, The Chickasaws, 109–11.

31 Gibson, The Chickasaws, 108–11.

32 Button and Provenzo, History of Education and Culture in America, 125–26.

33 Adams, Education for Extinction; Cremin, American Education: The National Experience; Ellis, To Change Them Forever; McBeth, Ethnic Identity and the Boarding School Experience; Spring, The American School.

34 Gibson, The Chickasaws, 111.

35 Oberly, Lake Mohonk Conference proceedings, 1885.

36 Gibson, The Chickasaws, 112.

37 Gibson, The Chickasaws, 112.

38 Button and Provenzo, History of Education and Culture in America, 67–70; Spring, The American School.

39 Gibson, The Chickasaws, 113, 117.

40 Anson Gleason, quoted in Missionary Herald, vol. 26, 1830, 383.

41 M. Wright, Indian Tribes of Oklahoma, 96.

42 Gibson, The Chickasaws, 120.

43 Prucha, Documents in United States Indian Policy, 52–53.

44 Cremin, American Education: The National Experience, 245.

45 G. Foreman, Indian Removal, 198; Gibson, The Chickasaws, 126.

46 G. Foreman, Indian Removal, 201; Gibson, The Chickasaws, 154.

47 Homer, Treaty of 1834, Constitution and Laws of the Chickasaw Nation, 463; Treaty of 1832, 453.

48 Homer, Treaty of 1837, Constitution and Laws of the Chickasaw Nation, 474–77.

49 M. Wright, Indian Tribes of Oklahoma, 89.

50   Gibson, The Chickasaws, 207.

51   G. Foreman, The Five Civilized Tribes, 140; Gibson, The Chickasaws, 199–200.

52   M. Wright, Indian Tribes of Oklahoma, 89.

53   Gibson, The Chickasaws, 176.

54   G. Foreman, Indian Removal, 218; Gibson, The Chickasaws, 176–77.

55   G. Foreman, Indian Removal, 218–19.

56   Gibson, The Chickasaws, 189.

57   M. Wright, Indian Tribes of Oklahoma, 90.

58   M. Wright, Indian Tribes of Oklahoma.

59   Homer, Treaty of 1855, Constitution and Laws of the Chickasaw Nation, 482–95.

60   Gibson, The Chickasaws, 192–99.

61   M. Wright, Indian Tribes of Oklahoma, 91.

62   C. Foreman, "Education among the Chickasaw Indians," 142, 155.

63   C. Foreman, "Education among the Chickasaw Indians," 163.

64   Office of Indian Affairs, School File B 432–568, Norwich, Connecticut, 1849, B-568, M234, Letters Received by the Office of Indian Affairs, 1824–1880, Microfilm Roll 784, National Archives, Washington DC.

65   Street, Social Literacies, 36.

3. Chickasaw Girls' School

 1   Carr, "Bloomfield Academy and Its Founder," 368.

 2   Carr, "Bloomfield Academy and Its Founder," 369.

 3   Carr, "Bloomfield Academy and Its Founder," 368.

 4   Carr, "Bloomfield Academy and Its Founder," 369.

 5   Carr, "Bloomfield Academy and Its Founder," 368–69.

 6   Spring, The American School, 97–103.

 7   Peterson, "Patient and Useful Servants," 105.

 8   Hobbs, Nineteenth-Century Women Learn to Write, 14.

 9   Peterson, "Patient and Useful Servants," 113.

10   Carr, "Bloomfield Academy and Its Founder," 372–73.

11   Carr, "Bloomfield Academy and Its Founder," 369.

12   Carr, "Bloomfield Academy and Its Founder," 373–74.

13   Carr, "Bloomfield Academy and Its Founder," 372.

14   J. Jackson, "Survey of Education in Eastern Oklahoma," 205.

15   Hiemstra, "Presbyterian Mission Schools among the Choctaws and Chickasaws," 36.

16   Cremin, American Education: The National Experience, 234.

17   Button and Provenzo, History of Education and Culture in America, 40.

18   Spring, *The American School*, 21; Button and Provenzo, *History of Education and Culture in America*, 38.

19   Button and Provenzo, *History of Education and Culture in America*, 19.

20   Spring, *The American School*, 17, 21.

21   Button and Provenzo, *History of Education and Culture in America*, 39.

22   Cremin, *American Education: The National Experience*, 67.

23   Carr, "Bloomfield Academy and Its Founder," 369.

24   Peterson, "Patient and Useful Servants," 119.

25   Carr, "Bloomfield Academy and Its Founder," 369–70.

26   Carr, "Bloomfield Academy and Its Founder," 370.

27   Carr, "Bloomfield Academy and Its Founder," 370.

28   Harriet Byrd to Reverend Dr. Sehan, 3 April 1857, and Lorena Factor to Reverend Dr. Sehan, 2 April 1857, Indian Mission Conference Reports, Louisville, Kentucky, 1857, quoted in Hall, "Bloomfield Indian School and Its Work," 13–14.

29   Angelina Hosmer Carr to Reverend Dr. Sehan, 2 April 1857, Indian Mission Conference Reports, Louisville, Kentucky, quoted in Hall, "Bloomfield Indian School and Its Work," 14.

30   Peterson, "Patient and Useful Servants," 106.

31   Cremin, *American Education: The National Experience*, 234.

32   Crawford, *Annual Report of the Commissioner of Indian Affairs*, 11.

33   Carr, "Bloomfield Academy and Its Founder," 372, 373.

34   Carr, "Bloomfield Academy and Its Founder," 371–72.

35   Mitchell, "Bloomfield Academy," 414.

36   Carr, "Bloomfield Academy and Its Founder," 372.

37   M. Wright, *Indian Tribes of Oklahoma*, 92.

38   Carr, "Bloomfield Academy and Its Founder," 372, 374.

39   Clegg and Oden, *Oklahoma Methodism in the Twentieth Century*, 31.

40   Carr, "Bloomfield Academy and Its Founder," 375.

41   Clegg and Oden, *Oklahoma Methodism in the Twentieth Century*, 32–34.

42   Mitchell, "Bloomfield Academy," 412.

43   Homer, Treaty of 1866, *Constitution and Laws of the Chickasaw Nation*, 495–519.

44   M. Wright, *Indian Tribes of Oklahoma*, 92.

45   Hall, "Bloomfield Indian School and Its Work," 19.

46   "History of School," *A Century of Progress: Bloomfield 1852–Carter 1952* (special ed. of Bloomfield yearbook), Bloomfield School Documents File, File 70.96.8, Chickasaw Council House Museum, Tishomingo OK, 2–3.

47   Carr, "Bloomfield Academy and Its Founder," 377.

48   *The Vindicator*, New Boggy, Choctaw Nation, Indian Territory, 14 June 1873.

49　Homer, *Constitution and Laws of the Chickasaw Nation*, 98–99.

50　Hall, "Bloomfield Indian School and Its Work," 20.

51　Homer, *Constitution and Laws of the Chickasaw Nation*, 98, 125–26.

52　Message of Governor Benjamin Crooks Burney to the Chickasaw Legislature, 1 September 1879, in *Cherokee Advocate*, Tahlequah, Cherokee Nation, Indian Territory, 24 September 1879.

53　Carr, "Bloomfield Academy and Its Founder," 377.

54　Homer, *Constitution and Laws of the Chickasaw Nation*, 207–8, 368–69.

55　"History of School," Bloomfield School Documents File, 4.

56　"History of School," Bloomfield School Documents File, 4.

57　"A Trip to Bloomfield: Graduating Exercises at the Young Ladies' Seminary," *Denison (Texas) Gazette*, 28 June 1896.

58　Carr, "Bloomfield Academy and Its Founder," 378; Homer, *Constitution and Laws of the Chickasaw Nation*.

59　Carr, "Bloomfield Academy and Its Founder," 378; Homer, *Constitution and Laws of the Chickasaw Nation*.

60　Mitchell, "Bloomfield Academy," 419; 1898 Grade Records, Bloomfield School Documents File, Bloomfield Scrapbook, P60, Chickasaw Council House Museum, Tishomingo OK.

61　Hall, "Bloomfield Indian School and Its Work," 37.

62　"A Trip to Bloomfield," *Denison (Texas) Gazette*.

63　Mitchell, "Bloomfield Academy," 412, 424, 420.

64　Hobbs, *Nineteenth-Century Women Learn to Write*, 1.

65　1885 Monthly Report of Scholastic Standing for January, 1898 Grade Records, Bloomfield School Documents File, Bloomfield Scrapbook, P60, Chickasaw Council House Museum, Tishomingo OK.

66　Mitchell, "Bloomfield Academy," 419.

67　Bloomfield Letterheads, Official, Bloomfield Academy File, File 30, Chickasaw Council House Museum, Tishomingo OK.

68　Hall, "Bloomfield Indian School and Its Work," 37–38.

69　Welter, "The Cult of True Womanhood," 152.

70　Bloomfield Poetry, Bloomfield Academy File, File 34, Chickasaw Council House Museum, Tishomingo OK.

71　Mitchell, "Bloomfield Academy," 421, 420.

72　"History of School," Bloomfield School Documents File, 4; Mitchell, "Bloomfield Academy," 419.

73　Mitchell, "Bloomfield Academy," 420.

74　Mitchell, "Bloomfield Academy," 420–21.

75   1904 Commencement Program, Bloomfield Academy File, File 26, Chickasaw Council House Museum, Tishomingo OK.

76   Mitchell, "Bloomfield Academy," 423.

77   1904 Quarterly Report, Bloomfield Reports, Bloomfield Academy File, File 35, Chickasaw Council House Museum, Tishomingo OK.

78   "A Trip to Bloomfield," Denison (Texas) Gazette.

79   1904 Commencement Program, Bloomfield Academy File.

80   J. Jackson, "Survey of Education in Eastern Oklahoma," 201.

81   J. Jackson, "Survey of Education in Eastern Oklahoma," 201.

82   J. Jackson, "Survey of Education in Eastern Oklahoma," 202.

4. The Women's Story

1   Prucha, American Indian Policy in Crisis, 228.

2   Prucha, Documents of United States Indian Policy, 171–72.

3   Prucha, American Indian Policy in Crisis, 255, 374.

4   Prucha, American Indian Policy in Crisis, 375–77, 380.

5   Prucha, Documents of United States Indian Policy, 170.

6   Prucha, American Indian Policy in Crisis, 190–95.

7   Prucha, Documents of United States Indian Policy, 197–98.

8   Gibson, The Chickasaws, 272.

9   Lomawaima, They Called It Prairie Light, 37.

10   Prucha, American Indian Policy in Crisis, 263.

11   Gibson, The Chickasaws, 267, 276–78.

12   Hirschfelder and Kreipe de Montano, eds., The Native American Almanac, 23.

13   C. Foreman, "Chickasaw Manual Labor Academy," 354.

14   Prucha, Documents of United States Indian Policy, 180–81.

15   "History of School," Bloomfield School Documents File, 4.

16   Hall, "Bloomfield Indian School and Its Work," 50.

17   "Bloomfield Seminary Edition," Oklahoma Indian School Magazine 1 (September 1932): 5–25, esp. p. 9, William A. McGalliard Collection, 1109, Ardmore Public Library, Ardmore OK.

18   "Bloomfield Seminary Edition," 18–20, 24–25, William A. McGalliard Collection; Hall, "Bloomfield Indian School and Its Work," 56.

19   Hall, "Bloomfield Indian School and Its Work," 55, 57.

20   Hall, "Bloomfield Indian School and Its Work," 54–56.

21   Hettie McCauley King, interview, 2–6. Note that here and in subsequent interviews the numbers refer to the page numbers in the interview transcripts.

22   Juanita Keel Tate, interview, 4–5.

23 Frances Griffin Robinson, interview, 2.

24 Fannye Williford Skaggs and Leona Williford Isaac, interview, 6.

25 Mary Pittman Parris, Clara Pittman Gatlin, and Ula Mae Pittman Welch, interview, 2–7.

26 Prucha, Documents of United States Indian Policy, 181.

27 Frances Griffin Robinson, interview, 30.

28 Fannye Williford Skaggs and Leona Williford Isaac, interview, 42.

29 Mary Pittman Parris, Clara Pittman Gatlin, and Ula Mae Pittman Welch, interview, 30, 45–46.

30 Claudine Williford King, interview, 21–22.

31 Leona Williford Isaac, interview, 42.

32 Prucha, Documents of United States Indian Policy, 174–75.

33 Leona Williford Isaac, interview, 42.

34 Fanny Hughes Bass, interview, 5.

35 Claudine Williford King, interview, 12.

36 Jeanne Liddell Cochran, interview, 16–17.

37 Ida Bell Hughes Martin, interview, 5.

38 Dorothy Wall Holt, interview, 5.

39 Juanita Keel Tate, interview, 7.

40 Jeanne Liddell Cochran, interview, 3.

41 Prucha, Documents of United States Indian Policy, 181.

42 Ora Lee Chuculate Woods, interview, 15.

43 Juanita Keel Tate, interview, 10.

44 Dorothy Wall Holt, interview, 22.

45 Dorothy Wall Holt, interview, 22.

46 Juanita Keel Tate, interview, 11–12.

47 Mary Pittman Parris, Clara Pittman Gatlin, and Ula Mae Pittman Welch, interview, 28–29.

48 Hillary Rodham Clinton, address at celebration in honor of the Sacajewa coin and American Indian and Alaskan Native women, 4 May 1999, Washington DC.

49 Prucha, Documents of United States Indian Policy, 218.

50 Pauline Williford Adkins, interview, 28.

51 Francis Griffin Robinson, interview, 18.

52 Jeanne Liddell Cochran, interview, 19.

53 Mary Pittman Parris, Clara Pittman Gatlin, and Ula Mae Pittman Welch, interview, 16.

54 Hall, "Bloomfield Indian School and Its Work," 49, 50.

55 Hall, "Bloomfield Indian School and Its Work," 51.

56 "History of School," Bloomfield School Documents File, 4.

57   Hall, "Bloomfield Indian School and Its Work," 53.

58   "History of School," Bloomfield School Documents File, 4.

59   "History of School," Bloomfield School Documents File, 4.

60   "Bloomfield Seminary Edition," William A. McGalliard Collection, 9.

61   "History of School," Bloomfield School Documents File, 5.

62   "Bloomfield Seminary Edition," William A. McGalliard Collection, 15.

63   Hall, "Bloomfield Indian School and Its Work," 59, 60.

64   Dorothy Wall Holt, interview, 18–19.

65   Jeanne Liddell Cochran, interview, 13.

66   Fannye Williford Skaggs and Leona Williford Isaac, interview, 56.

67   Claudine Williford King, interview, 14.

68   Pauline Williford Adkins, interview, 10.

69   Oral Lee Chuculate Woods, interview, 24.

70   Mary Pittman Parris, Clara Pittman Gatlin, and Ula Mae Pittman Welch, interview, 19–20.

71   Juanita Keel Tate, interview, 20.

72   "Bloomfield Seminary Edition," William A. McGalliard Collection, 25.

73   Juanita Keel Tate, interview, 8.

74   Pauline Williford Adkins, interview, 26.

75   "Bloomfield Seminary Edition," William A. McGalliard Collection, 15–17.

76   Claudine Williford King, interview, 25.

77   Claudine Williford King, interview, 17–20.

78   Claudine Williford King, interview, 17–20.

79   Jeanne Liddell Cochran, interview, 30–46.

80   "Bloomfield Seminary Edition," William A. McGalliard Collection, 17.

81   Fannye Williford Skaggs and Leona Williford Isaac, interview, 19.

82   Pauline Williford Adkins, interview, 14–15.

83   "Bloomfield Seminary Edition," William A. McGalliard Collection, 17.

84   Ula Mae Pittman Welch, interview, 26.

85   Fannye Williford Skaggs and Leona Williford Isaac, interview, 14–15.

86   Jeanne Liddell Cochran, interview, 23–24.

87   "Bloomfield Seminary Edition," William A. McGalliard Collection, 17.

88   "Bloomfield Seminary Edition," William A. McGalliard Collection, 19–20.

89   Frances Griffin Robinson, interview, 11.

90   Ula Mae Pittman Welch, interview, 23–24.

91   "Bloomfield Seminary Edition," William A. McGalliard Collection, 19–20.

92   Mary Pittman Parris, Clara Pittman Gatlin, and Ula Mae Pittman Welch, interview, 23–24.

93   "Bloomfield Seminary Edition," William A. McGalliard Collection, 20–22.

94 "Bloomfield Seminary Edition," William A. McGalliard Collection, 25.

95 Eleanor Allen, Letter to Parents, 5 August 1919, Bloomfield Academy File, File 32, Chickasaw Council House Museum, Tishomingo OK.

96 Claudine Williford King, interview, 23.

97 Fannye Williford Skaggs and Leona Williford Isaac, interview, 28.

98 Mary Pittman Parris, Clara Pittman Gatlin, and Ula Mae Pittman Welch, interview, 14.

99 Ula Mae Pittman Welch, interview, 14.

100 Mary Pittman Parris, Clara Pittman Gatlin, and Ula Mae Pittman Welch, interview, 38.

101 Frances Griffin Robinson, interview, 8.

102 Jeanne Liddell Cochran, interview, 10–13.

103 Pauline Williford Adkins, interview, 21.

104 1928 commencement program, reproduced in Hall, "Bloomfield Indian School and Its Work," 61.

105 Ora Lee Chuculate Woods, interview, 3–10.

106 Claudine Williford King, interview, 34–37.

107 Dorothy Wall Holt, interview, 28–33.

108 Frances Griffin Robinson, interview, 32–34.

109 Juanita Keel Tate, interview, 14–15.

110 Ora Lee Chuculate Woods, interview, 18.

111 Hettie McCauley King, interview, 24.

112 Dorothy Wall Holt, interview, 31.

113 Claudine Williford King, interview, 31.

114 Jeanne Liddell Cochran, interview, 44–47.

115 Dorothy Wall Holt, interview, 34–35.

116 Pauline Williford Adkins, interview, 35–36.

117 Jeanne Liddell Cochran, interview, 44–47.

118 Juanita Keel Tate, interview, 20.

119 Frances Griffin Robinson, interview, 43.

120 Fannye Williford Skaggs and Leona Williford Isaac, interview, 44–45.

121 Claudine Williford King, interview, 32.

122 Mary Pittman Parris, Clara Pittman Gatlin, and Ula Mae Pittman Welch, interview, 18.

5. To End the Story

1 Devon Mihesuah, *Cultivating the Rosebuds*, 115.

2 Claudine Williford King, interview, 40–41.

3 Frances Griffin Robinson, interview, 34–35.

4   Jeanne Liddell Cochran, interview, 5–6.

5   Hettie McCauley King, interview, 7.

6   Dorothy Wall Holt, interview, 33.

7   Pauline Williford Adkins, interview, 34.

8   Ora Lee Chuculate Woods, interview, 19.

9   Leona Williford Isaac and Fannye Williford Skaggs, interview,59–62.

10 Pauline Williford Adkins, interview, 40.

11 Clara Pittman Gatlin, Mary Pittman Parris, and Ula Mae Pittman Welch, interview, 37–38.

12 Claudine Williford King, interview, 45.

Bibliography

Interviews and Manuscript Materials

Interviews

Adkins, Pauline Williford. Interview by author. Tape and video recording. Ardmore OK, 17 June 1996.

Bass, Fanny Hughes. Interview by author. Tape and video recording. Tishomingo OK, 14 June 1996.

Cochran, Jeanne Liddell. Interview by author. Tape and video recording. Marietta OK, 29 June 1995.

Gatlin, Clara Pittman. Interview by author. Tape and video recording. Durant OK, 22 July 1996.

Holt, Dorothy Wall. Interview by author. Tape and video recording. Ardmore OK, 28 June 1996.

Isaac, Leona Williford. Interview by author. Tape and video recording. Moore OK, 8 July 1996.

Kemp, Betty Ruth. Interview by author. Tape and video recording. Norman OK, 16 July 1996.

King, Claudine Williford. Interview by author. Tape and video recording. Newkirk OK, 20 July 1996.

King, Hettie McCauley. Interview by author. Tape and video recording. Ardmore OK, 29 June 1996.

Martin, Ida Bell Hughes. Interview by author. Tape and video recording. Tishomingo OK, 14 June 1996.

Parris, Mary Pittman. Interview by author. Tape and video recording. Durant OK, 22 July 1996.

Robinson, Frances Griffin. Interview by author. Tape and video recording. Lebanon OK, 7 July 1996.

Skaggs, Fanny Williford. Interview by author. Tape and video recording. Moore OK, 8 July 1996.

Tate, Juanita Keel. Interview by author. Tape and video recording. Ardmore OK, 23 June 1996.

Welch, Ula Mae Pittman. Interview by author. Tape and video recording. Durant OK, 22 July 1996.

Woods, Ora Lee Chuculate. Interview by author. Tape and video recording. Durant OK, 15 July 1996.

Manuscript Materials

Bloomfield Academy File. Chickasaw Council House Museum, Tishomingo OK.

Bloomfield School Documents File. Chickasaw Council House Museum, Tishomingo OK.

William A. McGalliard Collection. Ardmore Public Library, Ardmore OK.

National Archives, Washington DC.

Lake Mohonk Conference of Friends of the Indians (1883–1929). Annual proceedings originally published by Indian Rights Association and also available on microfilm at State Historical Society of Wisconsin Library, Madison.

Published Sources

Adair, James. *The History of the American Indians*. 1775. Reprint, New York: Johnson Reprint, 1968.

Adams, David Wallace. *Education for Extinction: American Indians and the Boarding School Experience, 1875–1928*. Lawrence: UP of Kansas, 1995.

Allen, Paula Gunn. *The Sacred Hoop: Recovering the Feminine in American Indian Traditions*. Boston: Beacon Press, 1986.

Balyeat, Frank A. "Joseph Samuel Murrow, Apostle to the Indians." *Chronicles of Oklahoma* 35 (autumn 1957): 297–313.

Barton, David. *Literacy: An Introduction to the Ecology of Written Language*. Cambridge MA: Blackwell, 1994.

Bataille, Gretchen, and Kathleen Mullen Sands. *American Indian Women: Telling Their Lives*. Lincoln: U of Nebraska P, 1984.

Berkhofer, Robert F., Jr. *Salvation and the Savage: An Analysis of Protestant Missions and American Indian Response, 1787–1862*. New York: Atheneum Press, 1976.

——. *The White Man's Indian: Images of the American Indian from Columbus to the Present*. New York: Knopf, 1978.

Berlin, James A. *Rhetoric and Reality: Writing Instruction in American Colleges, 1900–1985*. Carbondale: Southern Illinois UP, 1987.

Botkin, Sam L. "Indian Missions of the Episcopal Church in Oklahoma." *Chronicles of Oklahoma* 36 (spring 1958): 40–47.

Brown, Dee. *Bury My Heart at Wounded Knee: An Indian History of the American West.* New York: Holt, Rinehart and Winston, 1970.

Brown, Opal Hartsell. *Indomitable Oklahoma Women.* Oklahoma City: Western Heritage Books, 1994.

Bryce, J. Y. "Beginnings of Methodism in Indian Territory, 1815–1855." *Chronicles of Oklahoma* 7 (December 1929): 475–86.

——. "Some Historical Items of Interest." *Chronicles of Oklahoma* 7 (September 1929): 337–39.

——. "Some Notes of Interest concerning Early Day Operations in Indian Territory by Methodist Church South." *Chronicles of Oklahoma* 4 (September 1926): 233–41.

Burwell, Jason O. "Chickasaw Woman Recalls Discipline." *Chickasaw Times,* June 1994, 4–5.

Button, H. Warren, and Eugene F. Provenzo, Jr. *History of Education and Culture in America.* Englewood Cliffs NJ: Prentice Hall, 1983.

Carr, Sarah J. "Bloomfield Academy and Its Founder." *Chronicles of Oklahoma* 2, no. 4 (December 1924): 365–79.

Child, Brenda J. *Boarding School Seasons: American Indian Families, 1900–1949.* Lincoln: U of Nebraska P, 1998.

Chisolm, Bishop Johnnie. "Harley Institute." *Chronicles of Oklahoma* 4, no. 2 (1926): 116–28.

Clegg, Leland, and William B. Oden. *Oklahoma Methodism in the Twentieth Century.* Nashville: Parthenon Press, 1968.

Coleman, Michael C. *American Indian Children at School, 1850–1930.* Jackson: UP of Mississippi, 1993.

Cotterill, R. S. *The Southern Indians: The Story of the Civilized Tribes before Removal.* Norman: U of Oklahoma P, 1954.

Crawford, Thomas Hartley. *Annual Report of the Commissioner of Indian Affairs.* 28th Cong., 2d sess., 1844.

Cremin, Lawrence A. *American Education: The Colonial Experience, 1607–1783.* New York: Harper and Row, 1970.

——. *American Education: The National Experience, 1783–1876.* New York: Harper and Row, 1980.

Cushman, H. B. *History of the Choctaw, Chickasaw and Natchez Indians.* Greenville TX, 1899. Reprint, ed. Angie Debo. Norman: U of Oklahoma P, 1999.

Davis, Carolyn. "Education of the Chickasaws." *Chronicles of Oklahoma* 15 (December 1937): 415–48.

Debo, Angie. *And Still the Waters Run.* New York: Gordian Press, 1966.

———. *A History of the Indians of the United States*. Norman: U of Oklahoma P, 1970.

Deloria, Vine Deloria, Jr., ed. *American Indian Policy in the Twentieth Century*. Norman: U of Oklahoma P, 1985.

Dippie, Brian W. *The Vanishing American: White Attitudes and U.S. Indian Policy*. Lawrence: UP of Kansas, 1982.

Ellis, Clyde. *To Change Them Forever: Indian Education at the Rainy Mountain Boarding School, 1893–1920*. Norman: U of Oklahoma P, 1996.

Foreman, Carolyn Thomas. "The Balentines, Father and Son, in the Indian Territory." *Chronicles of Oklahoma* 34 (winter 1956–57): 417–29.

———. "The Cherokee Gospel Tidings of Dwight Mission." *Chronicles of Oklahoma* 12 (December 1934): 454–69.

———. "Chickasaw Manual Labor Academy." *Chronicles of Oklahoma* 23 (winter 1945–46): 338–57.

———. "Education among the Chickasaw Indians." *Chronicles of Oklahoma* 15 (June 1937): 139–65.

———. "Fairfield Mission." *Chronicles of Oklahoma* 27 (winter 1949–50): 373–88.

———. "Israel G. Vore and Levering Manual Labor School." *Chronicles of Oklahoma* 25 (autumn 1947): 198–217.

———. "Mary C. Greenleaf at Wapanucka Female Manual Labor School." *Chronicles of Oklahoma* 24 (spring 1946): 26–39.

———. "New Hope Seminary, 1844–1897." *Chronicles of Oklahoma* 22 (autumn 1944): 271–99.

Foreman, Grant. "Dwight Mission." *Chronicles of Oklahoma* 12 (March 1934): 42-51.

———. *The Five Civilized Tribes*. Norman: U of Oklahoma P, 1934.

———. *Indian Removal: The Emigration of the Five Civilzed Tribes of Indians*. 3d ed. Norman: U of Oklahoma P, 1972.

Freire, Paulo. *Pedagogy of the Oppressed*. Rev. ed. New York: Continuum, 1993.

Galloway, Patricia. *Choctaw Genesis, 1500–1700*. Lincoln: U of Nebraska P, 1995.

Garrett, Kathleen. "Worcester, the Pride of the West." *Chronicles of Oklahoma* 30 (winter 1952–53): 386–96.

Gee, James. *Social Linguistics and Literacies: Ideology in Discourses*. New York: Falmer Press, 1990.

Gibson, Arrell M. *The Chickasaws*. Norman: U of Oklahoma P, 1971.

Giroux, Henry. *Between Borders: Pedagogy and the Politics of Cultural Studies*. New York: Routledge, 1994.

———. *Critical Pedagogy, the State, and Cultural Studies*. Albany: State U of New York P, 1989.

Graff, Harvey J. *The Legacies of Literacy: Continuities and Contradictions in Western Culture and Society*. Bloomington: Indiana UP, 1987.

——. *The Literacy Myth: Literacy and Social Structure in the Nineteenth Century City*. London: Academic Press, 1979.

Gutek, Gerald L. *Education in the United States: An Historical Perspective*. Englewood Cliffs NJ: Prentice Hall, 1986.

Hale, Duane K., and Arrell M. Gibson. *The Chickasaw*. Indians of North America series, ed. Frank Porter. New York: Chelsea House, 1991.

Hall, Ralph J. "Bloomfield Indian School and Its Work." Master's thesis, Oklahoma Agricultural and Mechanical College, 1931. Bloomfield Academy File, File 96.24. Chickasaw Council House Museum, Tishomingo OK.

Heath, Shirley Brice. *Ways with Words: Language, Life, and Work in Communities and Classrooms*. New York: Cambridge UP, 1983.

Hiemstra, William L. "Presbyterian Mission Schools among the Choctaws and Chickasaws, 1845–1861." *Chronicles of Oklahoma* 27 (spring 1949): 33–40.

Hirschfelder, Arlene, and Martha Kreipe de Montano, eds. *The Native American Almanac*. Englewood Cliffs NJ: Prentice Hall, 1993.

Hobbs, Catherine, ed. *Nineteenth-Century Women Learn to Write*. Charlottesville: UP of Virginia, 1995.

Homer, Davis A. *Constitution and Laws of the Chickasaw Nation*. Parsons KS: Foley Railway Printing, 1899.

Horne, Esther, and Sally McBeth. *Essie's Story: The Life and Legacy of a Shoshone Teacher*. Lincoln: U of Nebraska P, 1998.

Hoxie, Frederick. *A Final Promise: The Campaign to Assimilate the Indians, 1880–1920*. New York: Cambridge UP, 1989.

Hudson, Charles M., ed. *Four Centuries of Southern Indians*. Athens: U of Georgia P, 1975.

——. *The Southeastern Indians*. Knoxville: U of Tennessee P, 1976.

Jackson, Helen Hunt. *A Century of Dishonor: A Sketch of the United States Government's Dealing with Some of the Indian Tribes*. 1881. Reprint, New York: Scholarly Press, 1972.

Jackson, Joe C. "Summer Normals in Indian Territory after 1898." *Chronicles of Oklahoma* 37 (autumn 1959): 307–29.

——. "Schools among the Minor Tribes in Indian Territory." *Chronicles of Oklahoma* 32 (spring 1954): 58–69.

——. "Survey of Education in Eastern Oklahoma from 1907 to 1915." *Chronicles of Oklahoma* 29 (summer 1951): 200–221.

Johnston, Basil H. *Indian School Days*. Norman: U of Oklahoma P, 1988.

Kagey, J. N. "Jones Academy." *Chronicles of Oklahoma* 4 (December 1926): 338-39.

Kehoe, Mary Urban, Sister, C.D.P., and Abbot Isidore Robot, O.S.B. "The Educational Activities of Distinguished Catholic Missionaries among the Five Civilized Tribes." *Chronicles of Oklahoma* 24 (summer 1946): 166–82.

Kenny, Maurice. *Tekonwatonti/Molly Brant*. Fredonia NY: White Pine Press, 1992.

Kintgen, Eugene R., Barry M. Kroll, and Mike Rose, eds. *Perspectives on Literacy*. Carbondale: Southern Illinois UP, 1988.

Kjaer, Jens Christian. "The Lutheran Mission at Oaks, Oklahoma." *Chronicles of Oklahoma* 28 (spring 1950): 42–51.

Knoblauch, C. H. "Literacy and the Politics of Education." In *The Right to Literacy*, ed. Andrea A. Lunsford, Helene Moglen, and James Slevin. New York: Modern Language Association of America, 1990.

La Flesche, Francis. *The Middle Five: Indian Schoolboys of the Omaha Tribe*. 1900. Reprint, Madison: U of Wisconsin P, 1963.

Lindsey, Lilah Denton. "Memories of the Indian Territory Mission Field." *Chronicles of Oklahoma* 36 (summer 1958): 181–98.

Litton, Gaston. *History of Oklahoma at the Golden Anniversary of Statehood*. New York: Lewis Historical Publishing, 1957.

Lomawaima, K. Tsianina. *They Called It Prairie Light: The Story of Chilocco Indian School*. Lincoln: U of Nebraska P, 1994.

Malone, James H. *The Chickasaw Nation: A Short Sketch of a Noble People*. Louisville KY: John P. Morton, 1922.

McBeth, Sally J. *Ethnic Identity and the Boarding School Experience of West- Central Oklahoma American Indians*. Washington DC: University Press of America, 1983.

McReynolds, Edwin C. *Oklahoma: A History of the Sooner State*. Norman: U of Oklahoma P, 1954.

McReynolds, Edwin C., Alice Marriott, and Estelle Faulconer. *Oklahoma: The Story of its Past and Present*. Rev. ed. Norman: U of Oklahoma P, 1971.

Meserve, John Bartlett. "Governor Benjamin Franklin Overton and Governor Benjamin Crooks Burney." *Chronicles of Oklahoma* 16 (June 1938): 221–33.

Message of Governor Benjamin Crooks Burney to the Chickasaw Legislature, 1 September 1879. *Cherokee Advocate*, Tahlequah, Cherokee Nation, Indian Territory, 24 September 1879.

Mihesuah, Devon A. *Cultivating the Rosebuds: The Education of Women at the Cherokee Female Seminary, 1851–1909*. Urbana: U of Illinois P, 1993.

——. " 'Let Us Strive Earnestly to Value Education Aright': Cherokee Female Seminarians as Leaders of a Changing Culture." In *Nineteenth-Century Women Learn to Write*, ed. Catherine Hobbs. Charlottesville: UP of Virginia, 1995.

Miller, Floyd E. "Hillside Mission." *Chronicles of Oklahoma* 4 (December 1926): 223–28.

Miller, Lona Eaton. "Wheelock Mission." *Chronicles of Oklahoma* 29 (autumn 1951): 314–23.

Milligan, Dorothy, ed. *The Indian Way: The Chickasaws*. Quanah TX: Nortex Press, 1976.

Mitchell, Irene B. "Bloomfield Academy." *Chronicles of Oklahoma* 49 (winter 1971–72): 412–26.

Moffitt, James W. "Early History of the Armstrong Academy." *Chronicles of Oklahoma* 21 (March 1943): 89–91.

Momaday, N. Scott. *The Names: A Memoir.* Tucson: U of Arizona P, 1976.

——. *The Way to Rainy Mountain.* Albuquerque: U of New Mexico P, 1969.

Morris, John W., Charles R. Goins, and Edwin C. McReynolds. *Historical Atlas of Oklahoma.* 3d ed. Norman: U of Oklahoma P, 1986.

Nieberding, Velma. "St. Agnes School of the Choctaws." *Chronicles of Oklahoma* 33 (autumn 1955): 183–92.

Norris, L. David. *A History of Southeastern Oklahoma State University since 1909.* Durant OK: Mesa Publishing, 1986.

"Notes and Documents." *Chronicles of Oklahoma* 34 (winter 1956–57): 484–502.

"Notes and Documents." *Chronicles of Oklahoma* 44 (summer 1966): 216–29.

Ortiz, Simon. *Woven Stone.* Tucson: U of Arizona P, 1992.

Parke, Frank E., and J. W. Leflore. "Some of Our Choctaw Neighborhood Schools." *Chronicles of Oklahoma* 4 (June 1926): 149–52.

Peterson, Susan. "Patient and Useful Servants: Women Missionaries in Indian Territory." In *Women in Oklahoma: A Century of Change,* ed. Melvena Thurman. Oklahoma City: Oklahoma Historical Society, 1982.

Prucha, Francis Paul. *American Indian Policy in Crisis: Christian Reformers and the Indian, 1865–1900.* Norman: U of Oklahoma P, 1976.

——, ed. *Americanizing the American Indians: Writings by the "Friends of the Indian," 1880–1900.* Cambridge: Harvard UP, 1973.

——. *The Churches and the Indian Schools, 1888–1912.* Lincoln: U of Nebraska P, 1979.

——, ed. *Documents in United States Indian Policy.* 2d ed. Lincoln: U of Nebraska P, 1990.

——. *The Great Father: The United States Government and the American Indians.* Abridged ed. Lincoln: U of Nebraska P, 1986.

——. *Indian Policy in the United States: Historical Essays.* Lincoln: U of Nebraska P, 1981.

Pulliam, John D. *History of Education in America.* 3d ed. Columbus OH: Charles E. Merrill, 1982.

Rex, Joyce A. "John Harpole Carr and the Bloomfield Academy, Panola County, Chickasaw Nation, Indian Territory." *Oklahoma GS Quarterly* 39, no. 1 (1994): 35–36.

Scribner, Sylvia. "Literacy in Three Metaphors." In *Perspectives on Literacy,* ed. Eugene R. Kintgen, Barry M. Kroll, and Mike Rose. Carbondale: Southern Illinois UP, 1988.

Skolnick, Sharon, and Manny Skolnick. *Where Courage Is like a Wild Horse: The World of an Indian Orphanage.* Lincoln: U of Nebraska P, 1997.

St. Jean, Wendy. "More than a Love Affair: Chickasaw Women and Their European Husbands in the Eighteenth Century." *Journal of Chickasaw History* 1 (spring 1995): 8–12.

Spring, Joel. *The American School, 1642–1993.* 3d ed. New York: McGraw-Hill, 1994.

Street, Brian V. *Literacy in Theory and Practice.* London: Cambridge UP, 1984.

———. Social Literacies: Critical Approaches to Literacy in Development, Ethnography, and Education. New York: Longman, 1995.

Strickland, Rennard. The Indians in Oklahoma. Norman: U of Oklahoma P, 1980.

Szasz, Margaret. Education and the American Indian: The Road to Self- Determination since 1928. 2d ed. Albuquerque: U of New Mexico P, 1977.

———. Indian Education in the American Colonies, 1607–1783. Albuquerque: U of New Mexico P, 1988.

Tchudi, Stephen, and Paul J. Morris. The New Literacy: Moving beyond the 3Rs. San Francisco: Jossey-Bass, 1996.

Tinnin, Ida Wetzel. "Educational and Cultural Influences of the Cherokee Seminaries." Chronicles of Oklahoma 37 (spring 1959): 59–67.

Trennert, Robert. Alternative to Extinction: Federal Indian Policy and the Beginnings of the Reservation System, 1847–1851. Philadelphia: Temple UP, 1975.

"A Trip to Bloomfield: Graduating Exercises at the Young Ladies' Seminary." Denison (Texas) Gazette, 28 June 1896.

Utley, Robert M. The Indian Frontier of the American West, 1846–1890. Albuquerque: U of New Mexico P, 1984.

Vitanza, Victor. "'Notes' towards Historiographies of Rhetorics; or, The Rhetorics of the Histories of Rhetorics: Traditional, Revisionary, and Sub/Versive." Pre/Text 8, no. 1–2 (1987): 64–124.

———. Writing Histories of Rhetoric. Carbondale: Southern Illinois UP, 1994.

Welter, Barbara. "The Cult of True Womanhood, 1820–1860." American Quarterly 18 (1966): 151–74.

West, C. W. Missions and Missionaries of Indian Territory. Muskogee OK: Muscogee Publishing, 1990.

The WPA Guide to 1930s Oklahoma. 2d ed. Lawrence: U of Kansas P, 1986.

Wright, J. Leitch, Jr. The Only Land They Knew: The Tragic Story of the American Indians in the Old South. New York: Free Press, 1981.

Wright, Muriel H. A Guide to the Indian Tribes of Oklahoma. Norman: U of Oklahoma P, 1951.

———. "Wapanucka Academy, Chickasaw Nation." Chronicles of Oklahoma 12 (December 1934): 402–31.

Index

Numbers in italics refer to illustrations, which fall on unnumbered pages following page 68; the unnumbered pages are therefore referenced by letter, 68a being the first page of the illustration section.